The
Destruction of
Hillary
Clinton

Susan Bordo

The Destruction of Hillary Clinton

MELVILLE HOUSE
BROOKLYN · LONDON

First Melville House Printing: April 2017

Melville House Publishing   8 Blackstock Mews
          46 John Street   and   Islington
       Brooklyn, NY 112 01   London N4 2BT

mhpbooks.com

facebook.com/mhpbooks

@melvillehouse

Library of Congress Cataloging-in-Publication Data

Names: Bordo, Susan, 1947- author.
Title: The destruction of Hillary Clinton / Susan Bordo.
Description: Brooklyn : Melville House, 2017. I Includes bibliographical
  references and index.
Identifiers: LCCN 2017006567 I ISBN 9781612196633 (hardback)
Subjects: LCSH: Clinton, Hillary Rodham--Public opinion. I Women presidential
  candidates--United States--History--21st century. I Presidential
  candidates--United States--History--21st century. I Presidents--United
  States--Election--2016. I Women--Political activity--United
  States--History--21st century. I United States--Politics and
  government--2009- I Right and left (Political science)--United
  States--History--21st century. I Sexism in political culture--United
  States--History--21st century. I Mass media--Political aspects--United
  States--History--21st century. I Public opinion--United
  States--History--21st century. I BISAC: POLITICAL SCIENCE / Political
  Process / Elections. I BIOGRAPHY & AUTOBIOGRAPHY / Political. I SOCIAL
  SCIENCE / Women's Studies.
Classification: LCC E887.C55 B66 2017 I DDC 973.932092--dc23
LC record available at https://lccn.loc.gov/2017006567

ISBN: 978-1-61219-663-3

Printed in the United States of America
10 9 8 7 6 5 4 3 2 1

For Cassie and Edward

Contents

The
Destruction of
Hillary
Clinton

Timeline of Key Events

Early Years

October 26, 1947: Hillary Diane Rodham born in Chicago, Illinois.

1965–1969: Attends Wellesley College, majoring in political science and psychology. Elected student body president in 1968.

May, 1969: Became the first student to address the graduating class at commencement. Her speech and picture featured in Life.

1969: Attends Yale Law School, meets Bill Clinton. She is one of 27 women in a school of 235.

May, 1973: Receives law degree from Yale.

1974: Appointed to House Judiciary Committee investigating Watergate. Teaches at University of Arkansas Law School.

October 11, 1975: Marries Bill Clinton.

1976: Joins Rose Law Firm. Bill Clinton elected attorney general of Arkansas.

1978: Bill Clinton elected governor of Arkansas.

February 27, 1980: Daughter Chelsea Victoria born in Little Rock.

1980: Bill Clinton defeated in re-election bid.

1982: Bill Clinton re-elected governor.

First Lady of the United States

October 3, 1991: Bill Clinton announces his run for
president of the United States.

January 26, 1992: Bill and Hillary Clinton appear
together on 60 Minutes to respond to Gennifer Flowers
story. Hillary says she is not just "sitting here like
some little woman standing by my man like Tammy
Wynette."

March 5, 1992: *The New York Review of Books* declares
Hillary "one of the most important scholar-activists of
the last two decades."

March 16, 1992: Nightline airs "Making Hillary Clinton
an Issue" special. Hillary says, "I suppose I could
have stayed home and baked cookies and had teas, but
what I decided to do was fulfill my profession, which I
entered before my husband was in public life."

November, 1992: Bill Clinton elected president.

January, 1993: Bill Clinton names Hillary chair of Health
Care Task Force.

April, 1994: Appointment of Independent Counsel to
investigate "Whitewater." Ken Starr replaces first
appointee Robert Fiske.

September 5, 1995: Delivers a speech at the United
Nations Fourth World Conference on Women,
declaring "women's rights are human rights and
human rights are women's rights."

January 1998: On NBC's *The Today Show,* she calls

investigation into Bill Clinton's relations with Monica Lewinsky the latest episode in a "vast right-wing conspiracy."

Political Ascent

January 3, 2001–January, 23 2009: Served two terms as United States Senator representing New York. Of particular note were her fund-raising and legislative efforts to help rebuild the city after 9/11.

October 11, 2002: Votes "yes" on U.S. Senate Iraq War Resolution.

January 21, 2007: Announces her run for president of the United States.

January 5, 2008: Obama remarks that Hillary Clinton is "likeable enough" during the final debate before the New Hampshire primary.

June 3, 2008: Barack Obama gains enough delegates to become presumptive nominee.

June 7, 2008: Hillary ends her campaign for presidency, tells supporters that "although we weren't able to shatter that highest, hardest glass ceiling this time, thanks to you, it has about 18 million cracks in it and the light is shining through like never before."

January 29, 2009: Nominated by Barack Obama to be the sixty-seventh U.S. secretary of state. Among her many accomplishments: rebuilding the image of the United States abroad.

January 23, 2013: Testifies to Senate Foreign Relations Committee about 2012 attack on Benghazi.

February 1, 2013: Steps down from the State Department

with an approval rating of 66 percent. Later that year, the National Archives updates their guidelines to say that agency employees should only use personal email accounts in "emergency situations."

March 3, 2015: Hillary's use, before the guidelines changed, of a private email address becomes public knowledge when reported in *The New York Times*. Clinton's team insists that she acted within the laws governing email use.

2016 Presidential Campaign

April 12, 2015: Announces her second run for president of the United States.

September 8, 2015: Apologizes on ABC News for her use of a private email server. "Even though it was allowed, I should've used two accounts. One for personal, one for work-related emails. That was a mistake."

October 13, 2015: First Democratic debate held in Las Vegas, Nevada, featuring five candidates (Lincoln Chafee, Clinton, Martin O'Malley, Bernie Sanders, and Jim Webb). Afterward, Clinton and Sanders spar about "shouting." Clinton's statement that "when women talk, some people think we're shouting" resonates with women.

October 22, 2015: Hillary Clinton makes her final appearance before the House Select Committee on Benghazi. The consensus among commentators is that she successfully defended herself against all charges, despite a day-long grilling.

January, 2016: Trump threatens to bring Bill Clinton's

past into the campaign if Hillary isn't "nice" to him.

February 1, 2016: Sanders suggests Clinton is not a "true progressive."

February 4, 2016: In debate with Sanders, Clinton says, "I never sent or received any classified material."

April, 22 2016: Trump appears on *Fox & Friends* and introduces the term "Crooked Hillary."

April 28, 2016: Donald Trump accuses Clinton of playing "the Woman Card"; she responds, "Deal Me In."

May 23, 2016: Sanders refers to Clinton as "the lesser of two evils."

May 26, 2016: State Department inspector general releases an eighty-three-page evaluation of email management that describes the system as antiquated and cumbersome.

May 29, 2016: Fact-checkers confirm that Clinton is more honest than any of her 2016 opponents.

June 2016: *The Wall Street Journal*/NBC Poll reports that 16 percent more respondents find Trump "more honest and straightforward" than Hillary Clinton.

June 3, 2016: Susan Sarandon says Hillary is "more dangerous than Trump."

June 8, 2016: Hillary Clinton secures the Democratic presidential nomination.

June 9, 2016: Obama endorses Hillary: "I don't think there's ever been someone so qualified to hold this office."

July 2, 2016: Clinton gives a voluntary interview to the FBI about her email arrangements. The next day, on *Meet the Press*, she states she had "been eager to do it and was pleased to have the opportunity to assist the department in bringing the review to a conclusion."

July 5, 2016: FBI director James Comey announces investigation could "not find a case that would support bringing criminal charges." He breaks with established protocol by adding, "there is evidence that they were extremely careless in their handling of very sensitive, highly classified information."

July 7, 2016: Questioned by Elijah Cummings and Matt Cartwright, Comey admits that Clinton acted "reasonably" in treating unmarked emails as unclassified.

July 12, 2016: Bernie Sanders endorses Hillary Clinton.

July 18–21, 2016: Republican National Convention held in Cleveland, Ohio.

July 19, 2016: Donald Trump secures the Republican presidential nomination.

July 23, 2016: WikiLeaks releases 20,000 emails from the Democratic National Committee.

July 25–28, 2016: Democratic National Convention held in Philadelphia, Pennsylvania.

August 25, 2016: Hillary delivers speech in Las Vegas detailing Trump campaign's ties to the "alt-right" and white supremacists.

August 30, 2016: *The New York Times* publishes an editorial calling for the complete shut down of the Clinton Foundation.

September 10, 2016: Half of Hillary's comments about Trump's "basket of deplorables" widely disseminated in the media.

September 12, 2016: Clinton has pneumonia and tries to "power through it," causing GOP and media speculation about what she's "hiding."

September 26, 2016: First presidential general election
   debate held in Hempstead, New York. Hillary refers to
   Trump's bullying of Miss Universe Alicia Machado for
   gaining weight during her reign.

October 7, 2016: Tapes in which Trump brags to
   correspondent Billy Bush about groping women
   without their consent are leaked from *Access
   Hollywood.*

October 9, 2016: Second presidential general election
   debate held in St. Louis, Missouri.

October 14, 2016: Michelle Obama delivers impassioned
   speech about Trump's remarks in the *Access Hollywood*
   tapes, which she describes as having "shaken [her] to
   the core."

October 19, 2016: Third and final presidential general
   election debate held in Paradise, Nevada. Trump
   stages pre-debate media event with women whom he
   presents as having been abused by Bill Clinton. Under
   questioning by Anderson Cooper, Trump insists that
   the *Access Hollywood* tapes are just "locker room talk."
      Over the next two weeks, twelve women come
   forward with charges that Trump had groped them
   without consent. Many consider what happened to be
   sexual assault. As of this writing, the charges have not
   been investigated.

October 28, 2016: Eleven days before the election, James
   Comey breaks with the Department of Justice rules
   and issues a letter to Congress stating that the FBI
   will open a new investigation into recently discovered
   emails from Anthony Weiner's laptop, claiming that
   they "appear to be pertinent" to the FBI's previous

investigation of Clinton's private server. DOJ is strongly opposed to his action. The letter immediately goes public.

Clinton encourages Comey to release all the information the FBI has that led him to reopen the Clinton email investigation. "Let's get it all out," she says.

October 30, 2016: FBI obtains a warrant to examine the recently discovered emails.

Former attorney general Eric Holder writes an op-ed saying that Comey has "made a serious mistake."

November 4, 2016: Rudy Giuliani says he knew beforehand (from FBI agents) about the Weiner emails and Comey's plan to inform Congress.

Politico asks "a panel of activists, strategists, and operatives in eleven swing states" their opinions on the evolving 2016 presidential election campaign. Nearly two-thirds of Republicans say that FBI Director James Comey's October 28, 2016 letter announcing the reopening of the FBI's investigation into Clinton's emails "fundamentally altered the trajectory of the race."

November 6, 2016: James Comey issues a second letter to Congress, informing lawmakers that the review of emails from Anthony Weiner's computer was complete and that the investigation did not change the FBI's conclusion in July that neither Clinton nor her team had committed any prosecutable offenses.

November 8, 2016: Trump is elected president. Clinton, as we find out over the following two weeks, wins almost three million more popular votes than Trump.

November 25, 2016: Reports of Russian interference in the U.S. election begin to surface.

November 28, 2016: Trump claims, with no evidence, that "millions of people" voted illegally.

January 20, 2017: Trump is inaugurated president of the United States.

January 21, 2017: The Women's March on Washington and related protests around the world demonstrate peacefully for racial and gender equality, affordable healthcare, reproductive rights, and voting rights, generating record-breaking crowds.

Preface

This book is hard to write, as it requires revisiting events that caused me pain, anger, and frustration. I imagine memoir writers experience similar difficulty as they force themselves to reconstruct traumatic events from the past. But this book isn't a memoir, and many people would mock me for using the term "trauma" in connection with the events that I recall here. Yet for nearly a year I lived in a state of perpetual fury and helplessness. I often found myself waking up way too early, then falling asleep at unexpected times, not because I was sleepy but because consciousness felt like a burden.

Despite these characteristic symptoms, I wasn't suffering from something that happened to me—or, at least, not *only* to me. Thousands of people, in Facebook groups with names like "Hillary for President 2016" and "Feminists for Hillary," were experiencing much the same thing. Every morning, we'd visit each other's group pages and blogs, sharing and "liking" the articles that exposed the faux scandals, posting angry icons over the latest outrage on MSNBC's *Morning Joe*, and enjoying the freedom to be as enthusiastic as we wanted over a woman whom statistical polling, mainstream media reporting, and otherwise amiable neighbors had labeled one of the two most unpopular presidential candidates of all time.

Ours was a community bound by shared support for Hillary Clinton, but even more so by our amazement and distress over the disparity between the Hillary we were campaigning for and the Hillary we continually heard described as "deceptive," "untrustworthy," "unlikeable," and even "evil."

Bill Clinton, in his speech at the Democratic National Convention, described the "real" Hillary and another "made-up" one. Though I wouldn't use exactly those words, the juxtaposition is familiar to me, as my last book was about another flesh-and-blood woman who was replaced by a fiction. Her name was Anne Boleyn, and we know her in two different modes. One Anne Boleyn is the complex, good-and-bad Anne, second wife of Henry VIII, who made the fatal mistake of not staying in her proper wifely place and then getting on the wrong side of Thomas Cromwell; the other Anne Boleyn is a nasty caricature concocted by her political enemies and passed down through centuries via Catholic polemics, factually loose biographies, and sensationalizing novels, films, and television programs. That Anne is an overly ambitious, calculating, untrustworthy schemer who, while not always represented as guilty of adultery and treason (the crimes for which she was falsely charged), nonetheless got the fate she deserved. There's astonishingly little factual basis for this nasty version of Anne. She is a fantasy creation that lives within a narrative developed over time, one that turned politically motivated lies into inflammatory gossip and alchemized that gossip into what we now believe to be fact.

Today, with a twenty-four-hour news cycle that has gradually blurred the line between entertainment and information, it didn't take centuries for the real Hillary Clinton to be subjected to the same kind of poisonous alchemy. In a mere seventeen months, between the announcement of her candidacy in April of 2015 and the presidential election in November of 2016, the accomplished and poised former secretary of state Hillary Clinton turned into someone—or something—hardly recognizable. The features of this fictional creation, recycled over and over in newspaper articles and television reports, became familiar. Hillary was "flawed." "Untrustworthy." An uninspiring orator. Evasive. Not "available" enough to the media or "the people." "She thinks she's above the law." "She's in the pocket of Wall Street." "She thinks she's better than us." "Others would be in jail for the crimes she has committed." Or, perhaps most frequently, "There's just something about her I don't like." Even favorable op-eds and endorsements invariably qualified their praise of Hillary's qualifications with a nod to her imperfections as a candidate, and the "problems she had brought on herself."

Stepping back from the epithets and the scandal-mongering headlines, there is something mind boggling about the extreme contradictions between how millions of us view Hillary and the caricature that dominated the news during the election year.

Clinton's nearly three million popular vote margin over Trump demonstrate that whatever "mistrust" had become attached to her, whatever electoral force was exerted by those who wanted to "lock her up," there were powerful factors working in the opposite direction. Prior to running for president, she had a 66 percent approval rating. She ranked high (and still does) among the most admired women in the world. She was commended by politicians on both sides of the aisle for her ability to work with Republicans as well as members of her own party. Even one of her speeches—her famous Beijing "Women's rights are human rights" speech—

was ranked by American Rhetoric among the top one hundred American public speeches ever delivered.

The currently popular complaint against Clinton among Democrats is that she didn't communicate an effective "message" to the battleground "rust belt" states that ultimately decided the election. In terms of electoral numbers, those states were indeed key. But just why Clinton lost them isn't as clear as is now being presented. The emphasis on the demographics Clinton didn't appeal to also elides the importance of those groups she *did* appeal to: those for whom the fragility of human rights, always a priority for Clinton, was recognized as a "message" still needing to be delivered—perhaps especially so with Trump as the alternative.

"I had watched her when she was first lady of Arkansas," the late Maya Angelou told *The Guardian*. "I thought this white girl would come to Arkansas and play croquet on the lawn and throw tea parties. And she was just the opposite. She worked on public health and education . . . even prisons." During the 2016 election cycle, the mothers of Michael Brown, Trayvon Martin, Eric Garner, Tamir Rice, and Sandra Bland—who had lost children through police and other violence—found in Hillary a warm and fierce advocate, even before she announced her candidacy, and identified with Clinton's ability to "take a licking and keep on ticking."

Among some demographic groups—older blacks, for example—Hillary Clinton's "historic unpopularity" was an out-and-out falsehood; she won the black vote by 88 percent. Important civil-rights leaders such as John Lewis described their affection for her as that of a longstanding comrade-in-arms. "That determination and strength particularly has meaning to African American women," said Sharon Reed, sixty, a community-college teacher from North Charleston,

South Carolina. "Who has overcome more obstacles and darts and arrows than she has? And she's still standing and she's still strong."

These black mothers disputed the idea that Clinton was using them for political purposes, citing Clinton's long-standing work with Civil Rights activist and Children's Defense Fund founder Marian Wright Edelman, as well as other black community leaders. "I really got the sense that she could really relate to us, as being mothers and women and daughters," said Lucy McBath, whose teenage son, Jordan Davis, was shot and killed at a Jacksonville, Florida, gas station in 2012. Outreach director La Davia Drane described Clinton's connection to mothers, particularly black mothers, as "a secret sauce, it's a match made in heaven."

"I feel a kinship to who she is. She knows and understands the battle that we fight every day," said Ohio congresswoman Marcia Fudge. "She has a special place for us because she really gets it." On election night, an estimated 94 percent of black women voted for Clinton.

Clinton, like most politicians, was late to publicly support gay marriage. But members of the LGBTQ activist community remember her advocacy—mostly done without fanfare or media attention—in other ways: As soon as she began her tenure as secretary of state, she immediately got to work addressing a long list of discrimination complaints from LGBTQ staffers. She enacted a new rule making it easier for transgender people to register their identities on their passports by requiring only a doctor's note—a ruling that LGBTQ experts and advocates describe as "enormous," and "monumental." It was a change of tremendous practical value (eg, for travel abroad) and symbolic potency.

"It says, 'This proves who I am,' and it has the seal of the

United States on it," says Rick Garcia, founder of Equality Illinois and a longtime LGBTQ activist. During this election
cycle, Clinton ran the most LGBTQ-friendly presidential
campaign in U.S. history, incorporating acknowledgment of
LGBTQ accomplishments and issues into debate answers and
speeches, earning the endorsement (over Sanders) of all major
LGBTQ publications, organizations, and political action committees, and earning 78 percent of the LGBTQ vote. Her
courage in defying gender expectations also provided in-
spiration and support—for example, to writer and journalist
Jason Howard, who grew up in a rural, Eastern Kentucky
town and who found in First Lady Hillary a model of courage
and unconventionality, "who was rebelling against the status
quo in ways that [he] was only beginning to fathom": "Thir-
teen years old and closeted, unable to live openly in my small
Appalachian town where fundamentalist churches speckled
the landscape like a murder of crows, and preachers railed
against the abomination of deviant lifestyles . . . seeing Hillary Clinton more than hold her own in the patriarchal world
of politics gave me hope [and] made me realize that for people
like us—the ones destined to be outsiders in our culture—I
needed to find in myself the deep reservoir of strength and
sense of self that I saw in her."

And then, of course, there were the "older women," both
black and white—a group among which I include myself.
There's no way to know precisely how our support translated
in terms of votes, as the election results list divisions by age
and by gender, but not their intersection. There's no doubt,
however, that progressive baby-boomer women were unlikely
to dismiss gender as a negligible factor in the struggle for economic and social equality. "When we reach a certain age," as
Ginger McKnight-Chavers, a black, Harvard-educated lawyer,

describes it, "we become forgotten. For a mature woman of strength and intelligence to rise to represent and embody the voice of our nation would be inspirational to younger generations of women in ways in which they may not even imagine. But for more mature women, it would be transcendent."

Older women's support for Clinton was not only aspirational, it was also grounded in deep identification with where she was coming from. I'm just a few months older than Hillary, and have always felt a generational bond with her that transcends the differences in our backgrounds, personalities, and accomplishments. Baby boomers like us grew up during a historical transformation within which one cultural notion of what was required of girls was supplanted, virtually overnight, by another. During the 1950s, movies like *Father of the Bride* idealized the happy homemaker/good provider couple, and wartime industries put their efforts into selling them the latest kitchen appliances to complete the dream. There were teenage versions, too: kittenish child-women like Sandra Dee, with fluffy hair and bodies made for baby producing. It was all a glossy advertisement, of course, the selling of a dream purged of racial and ethnic variation, and one that few girls and women were economically able to attain. But as image and ideology, the "feminine mystique" (as Betty Friedan called it) was very real; it dominated the mass media, shaping (and often disappointing) expectations of parents, teachers, and employers—and the fantasies of many girls.

But, as our new Nobel Prize–winnng poet wrote, the times they were a-changin'. By the time I was sixteen, in 1963, I had become "political," and was ironing my hair and envying the girls who were tall, thin, and could play the guitar, like Mary Travers. As baby-boomer teenagers, girls were faced on a daily basis with the problem of straddling the happy homemaker fantasy and the new mystique of the "liberated woman" of the sixties. It was a constant push-pull, made all the more difficult by the fact that the gender restrictions—both legal and ideological—of the fifties were still very much in place. My first year at college, I watched a dorm mate nearly die from a botched illegal abortion. When I was sexually harassed by one of my teachers, I had no words to apply to the experience, only feelings of shame, anger, and the dismissive sentiments of my male friends: "Oh, Susan, don't be so sensitive." When I lost my scholarship to college, I saw nothing wrong with the reasoning that it was all well and good, as the funds could be used to keep a young man out of Vietnam. As a college dropout, I took a job as a clerk in a bookstore that paid forty-seven dollars a week, spent my nights sleeping around, and went on a hunt for the male person who would give meaning to my life.

On the face of it, my biography and Hillary Clinton's could not look more different. Hillary, by her own admission, had managed to escape, during her adolescence and young womanhood, many of the gender traps that I had fallen into. I picked my college—University of Chicago—for its reputation of being intellectually "avant-garde" and politically cutting-edge, full of the iconoclastic, long-haired rebel men that appealed to me at the time. Hillary, on the other hand, had been smart to choose an all-girl college—Wellesley—that "guaranteed a focus on academic achievement and extracurricular leadership we might have missed at a coed college" and "cleared out a lot of psychic space and created a safe zone for us to eschew appearances—in every sense of the word," as she recounted in *Living History*. Later, in law school, she fell in love with a man who truly did regard her as his equal, if not his superior. Bill Clinton, like Obama, has always maintained that he was "marrying up" to someone of greater intelligence and savvy than himself.

Yet, neither Hillary's brilliance, balance, or self-confidence could alter the cultural expectations or prohibitions of our generation. When Hillary went to take the law school admission test, as she told Henry Louis Gates:

> We had to go in to Harvard to take the test, and we were in a huge room, and there were very few women there, and we sat at these desks waiting for the proctors or whoever to come and all the young men around us started to harass us. They started to say, "What do you think you're doing? If you get into law school, you're going to take my position. You've got no right to do this. Why don't you go home and get married."

And when I read (in just what article or book I no longer remember) of how Hillary came crash-bang against the requirements of being the first lady of Arkansas a decade later—stop looking like a hippy, straighten your hair, put on some makeup, and for goodness sake, take your husband's last name—I understood the conflicts she faced as a more public, higher-stakes version of my own. When her husband began his first campaign for president, I wondered: How would this woman of my generation navigate what I knew would be a path too difficult for most of the rest of us?

I've been Hillary watching ever since she became someone newsworthy enough to follow. But until this election cycle, my tracking was sporadic—articles and notes shoved randomly in boxes. It was only because of Internet culture that a book like this became possible. At first, my social media posts were a sentence or two long, often accompanied by clips from TV shows and links to articles written by others: "I can't believe that Mika just said that!" "Thank goodness for Paul Krugman/Joy Reid/Peter Daou!" "This is reassuring news" (when a poll showed that if Trump were nominated, millennials would "flock to Clinton"). But I found I had a lot more to say than could be contained in a Facebook post, so I began to blog for *Huffington Post* and for a website of my own. Eventually, the result was a running, virtually daily record of the 2016 election and my reflections and analysis, from the primary, through the general, and ending in the election and its aftermath. Stitching that record together, ultimately, I discovered an answer—complex, multidimensional, and partaking of more outright political sabotage than I had expected—to the question that still keeps me up some nights, and that this book attempts to address. How could such an extraordinarily well-qualified, experienced, admired, accomplished candidate, whose victory seemed assured and would have been as unprecedented as that of Barack Obama's, come to be seen as a tool of the establishment, a chronic liar, and a talentless politician? How did this happen?

Introduction

In the early hours of Wednesday, November 9, 2016, the post-mortems began. Despite the polls that had favored Hillary for a decisive victory, Donald Trump had carried the Electoral College and won the 2016 presidential election. Television commentators, as shocked by the results as the rest of us, sprung somewhat awkwardly into pundit mode.

"What was missing in Hillary?" was how MSNBC's Chris Matthews put it to his panel of guests that night. "Where did she go wrong?" And over the next few weeks, on *Hardball* and other news shows, we got a variety of answers to that question:

"Overconfidence."

"The people wanted change."

"They weren't inspired."

"She didn't speak to the working class and their concerns."

"She couldn't connect."

"She had no economic message."

"She didn't resonate"

"She should have gone to Wisconsin."

"She should have gone to Michigan."

"She should have gone to Ohio."

Michael Moore, the filmmaker and activist who supported

Bernie Sanders in the primary and came out late in the day for Hillary in the general, declared decisively that she would have won the election if only she had told the press "I feel like crap" when she had pneumonia. Bernie would have done that, he said. The other panelists nodded and smiled. Matthews attempted an incompetent Brooklynese rendition of "I feel like crap," and the guys cracked up.

"If only they would have shown her more human side," Moore says, shaking his head. (In this book I'll address exactly why what Moore called "showing a human side" was not a viable option for Hillary.) A few weeks later, Moore would intensify his diagnosis and attribute Hillary's loss to her "disgraceful" campaign, which ignored the cries of "people like me" to visit the rust belt states.[1]

Bernie Sanders himself, without mentioning her name, implied that Hillary had botched the election by running a campaign on "identity politics." "It's not good enough for someone to say, 'I'm a woman! Vote for me!' What we need," he said on a book tour shortly after the election, "is a woman who has the guts to stand up to Wall Street, to the insurance companies, to the drug companies, to the fossil fuel industry." A few weeks later, he attributed Trump's win to the fact that the Democrats "didn't offer candidates and politicians [who] have the guts to stand up to the billionaire class and start representing the middle class and working families of America." Wonder what "gutless" candidate he imagined had failed to do the job?

1 In point of fact, Hillary Clinton was the first of all the presidential candidates to pay any attention to the water crisis in Flint, Michigan, collaborating with Flint mayor Karen Weaver in early January 2016—long before Sanders's visit on the eve of the Michigan primary, which he won only narrowly.

In fact, since the election, Sanders has done everything short of saying outright that had he been the nominee, the Democrats would have prevailed over Trump. Many of his supporters continue to believe the "myth that Sanders would have won" (as *Newsweek* senior editor Kurt Eichenwald calls it), despite the fact that in a campaign directed against him, Sanders would have run smack up against a brutal deluge of highly damaging opposition research. Clinton never ran that kind of campaign, at least in part for fear of alienating the young voters who were Sanders's base.

As for GOP responses to the election results, it was as if there had never been a "Never Trump" movement. Between November 2016 and January 2017, the president-elect was forgiven everything by the party—his many lies, his failure to produce his taxes or deal with conflicts of interests, even the *Access Hollywood* tapes that so offended other Republicans—while Trump himself attributed Hillary's nearly three-million-vote margin to election fraud via illegal immigrants (none of whom, apparently, were casting their fraudulent ballots in the states that would have given Hillary an electoral win).

In short, the two months in between the election and the inauguration were a festival of Hillary blaming, in which the Democrats participated as enthusiastically as the Republicans. Sometimes their criticisms were directed against "the party"—not entirely disingenuously, as Democrats are notorious self-flagellators—but even then, and even as her name was mentioned less and less over the following weeks, the "wrong messenger" was always implicit in Democrats' accusations.

The press, for the most part, went along with these diagnoses. "She couldn't escape being the wrong candidate for the political moment" (as Edward Isaac Dovere wrote in Politico) was the near-universal conclusion. Reading this, I wonder what an expression like "the political moment" could mean. Is this "moment" really only about the promise of jobs for white, working-class men in a few rust-belt states? Was there really such widespread dissatisfaction with the last eight years that people were hungry for "change"—any change? If any change was the goal then, sure, I can see how Trump might be framed as the "right" candidate for our "political moment," but the millions of people who have protested his administration both in this country and around the world suggest that the message of equality, which Hillary quite clearly promoted, is far from defunct. If anything, the "political moment" was more complex this year than in any other presidential campaign in history. If Hillary was so "wrong," what made her so wrong?

When, in response to the election results, Clinton or one of her representatives suggested a few other salient ingredients were being overlooked, those suggestions were usually derided: James Comey's revival, eleven days before the election, of public mistrust in Clinton over the email "scandal"? Don't be such a sore loser! Vladimir Putin's apparent connection to hacked material from the DNC? Impossible to measure! The massive right-wing industry in fake news, conspiracy theory, and Hillary-hate books? Politics as usual, and both sides were equally vicious. The lopsidedness of the Electoral College? Well, she should have played the game better.

And then there were those elements not mentioned at all: Bernie Sanders branding Hillary as the enemy of progressive politics, giving too many millennial voters the perception that Clinton was merely the tool of Wall Street and thereby splintering the Democratic vote by generation; the mainstream media's relentless emphasis on scandals that eventually came to nothing, and their repetition of narratives centered on Clinton's lack of popularity, lack of charisma, penchant for privacy, and "inauthenticity"; the media's justification: politics is about perception—or as it became fashionable to call it, "optics"—and it was their job to report on anything that contributed to the perceptions of voters. But keeping up with optics was a time- and attention-consuming business in this election cycle, with Clinton's political enemies continually tempting reporters with something suspicious, something that didn't look right, something Hillary must be hiding. In the mainstream media's rush to announce the latest rumors and attacks, fact-checking and context became sidebars left to investigative journalists whose findings rarely made headline news, leaving optics to rule as fact in the minds of many voters.

And, of course, there was the gender factor, which throughout Hillary's career has made her a living Rorschach test of people's nightmare images of female power. It's no surprise that as she came closer and closer to the most powerful position in the world, the misogyny directed toward her became increasingly vicious.

And it *was* vicious—almost medieval. During Hillary's campaign in 2008, the posters read "Iron My Shirts" and "Make Me A Sandwich"; in 2016 they called for putting "the bitch in jail" and pictured Hillary on a broomstick. I think this was in part a reflection of how the Internet, reality television, and, of course, the master of vilespeak himself, Donald Trump, had loosened the restraints on civil discourse. But also, more unadulterated fury seemed directed at Hillary than I had ever witnessed before.

While the rhetoric was ratcheted up in 2016, any mention

of sexism was dismissed—by some Democrats as well as most Republicans—as "playing the woman card." Many young people mistakenly considered women's issues passé; moderators largely ignored discrimination, equal pay, or reproductive rights in debates. Nor did we ever see a television-panel discussion of the sexist currents in the caricatures of Clinton as devious, overly ambitious, untrustworthy, and scheming. Throughout the 2016 election and in the postmortems that followed, "gender" and "sexism" were terms that seem to have been written in disappearing ink. (They re-emerged with a vengeance the day after Trump's inauguration.)

But while sexism was rarely invoked, it flourished without restraint when it came to assaults on Hillary Clinton's character, personality, and appearance. Indeed, it seemed to me (having followed the career of Hillary and other female politicians closely) that the undercurrent of anger against her in the 2016 election was unprecedented. It didn't start, or end, with Donald Trump's "crooked Hillary." True, we saw the most rabid, literal form of Hillary hate at the GOP convention. "We know she enjoys her pantsuits . . . What she deserves is a bright orange jumpsuit!" shouted Colorado's Darryl Glenn, to riotous applause. Chris Christie, on the second day of the convention, played prosecutor at a mock trial, calling out each of Hillary's "crimes" to delighted shouts of "Guilty! Guilty!" from the audience. Later in the convention, Ben Carson even invoked Lucifer. The crowds took every opportunity to chant "Lock her up!" The collective chant became such an eagerly anticipated feature of Trump rallies that they kept it going, even after post-election Trump, playing the beneficent pardoner (of someone who had actually committed no crimes), said he wouldn't continue to investigate the Clintons, who were such "nice people" and had "suffered so much" during the campaign. (Kellyanne Conway, Trump's campaign manager, added that she hoped it would help Hillary's "healing.")

It would be a mistake, however, to see the Hillary hatred that swelled during Trump's campaign as the main factor in the assault. Trump provided some incendiary mantras, but many Sanders supporters saw Hillary, at best, as the "lesser of two evils," and at worst as a "corporate whore." They harassed attendees at Clinton rallies and threw dollar bills at those heading for a Clinton fundraiser. Many members of the left-leaning media, irritated by both the notion that she was the "inevitable" nominee and by what they saw as her haughty avoidance of their probing, took every opportunity to celebrate Sanders's success and decry what they continually represented as Clinton's evasiveness. Among the GOP, those who had worked amicably with Hillary when she was a senator[2] and secretary of state subjected her to snarling interrogations worthy of a trial for witchcraft.

Between Sanders and the GOP witch-hunters, Hillary was blamed for every national disaster from racialized incarceration to the deaths of American diplomats during the raid on Benghazi. She was accused of having extraordinary powers that "enabled" her husband's infidelity, influenced Wall Street through the spell of a few polite remarks in public speeches, and put an entire nation in danger by "recklessly" handling classified material (that had not, in fact, been marked as clas-

---

2 As senator, Clinton formed working alliances to further health care and child protection issues with Tom DeLay, Newt Gingrich, Bill Frist, Robert Bennett, Rick Santorum, John Sununu, and Mike DeWine.

sified). Her vote alone, apparently, was responsible for the war in Iraq. She even had her own "familiar"—her husband—with whom she frequently merged, shape-shifting into a slithery, elusive man-woman called "The Clintons." This mythological creature lives by "rules of its own," and lines its pockets with the lucre amassed through a supposed "charity" foundation.

Oh, yes, and as secretary of state she had a private email server in her basement. Basement? Private? What else might have been going on there? A child pornography ring? Feminist covens? Animal sacrifice?

Does this picture sound like it belongs in a gruesomely illustrated version of a Grimm's fairy tale? It's a central premise of this book that the Hillary Clinton who was "defeated" in the 2016 election was, indeed, not a real person at all, but a caricature forged out of the stew of unexamined sexism, unprincipled partisanship, irresponsible politics, and a mass media too absorbed in "optics" to pay enough attention to separating facts from rumors, lies, and speculation. Of course, there was a flesh-and-blood woman there. But, like a reality show housewife, she was edited into a cartoon—with potent archetypal resonance. Cunning, deceptive, in league with the forces of greed and elitism over the "working people," fueled by personal ambition: that was the "Hillary Clinton" who hovered in the air of this election, not only at Trump rallies, but also in the rhetoric of many Sanders supporters, in the charges of the GOP interrogators who hammered away at her during neverending investigations into Benghazi and emails, and in the imaginations of those voters who voted for Trump (as one told Chris Hayes) simply "because he wasn't Hillary."

It's small consolation that now, with Trump in the White House, the absurdity of anyone finding Hillary the bigger liar, the more dangerous politician, or the greater friend to Goldman Sachs has become painfully and frighteningly apparent. Even so—or perhaps especially so now—the story of how such a bizarre chapter in American political history could come to be is worth telling.

1.

Dilemmas of the Female Politician

The Double Bind

There was a moment in the 2008 contest between Hillary Clinton and Barack Obama when it seemed that Obama—not usually one for "unforced errors"—had stepped into it. It was during the final debate, just before the New Hampshire primary, and Hillary, a highly accomplished debater, was answering questions as adroitly as usual. Then Scott Spradling, a news anchor at local TV station WMUR, took it to a more personal level:

"What can you say to the voters of New Hampshire, who see a resume and like it but are hesitating on the likability issue, where they seem to like Barack Obama more," he posed.

Hillary, surprising many, responded rather girlishly: "Well," she replied with a deliberately exaggerated pout, "that hurts my feelings." Then, with impeccable timing, she teased, "but I'll try to go on." She turned to Obama: "He's very likeable, I agree with that. I don't think I'm that bad."

Obama's reply—"You're likeable enough, Hillary"—seemed insensitive and cold to many viewers. It had been one of those rare moments when Hillary had publicly spoken about her feelings, and many women watching knew that she was being utterly—although perhaps inadvertently—"transparent." She was hurt, and she did find Obama likeable. Although it was delivered as though it was a joke, there was something be-seeching in that "I don't think I'm that bad" that reminded women of all the times they had fished for compliments, afraid to be seen as aggressive or demanding but craving reassur-ance. Obama's answer, clearly aimed at the politician instead of the woman, was oblivious to her vulnerability. For that one moment, he was the man who grudgingly tells his girlfriend "It looks okay" when she asks him if her butt looks too big in this dress.

The next morning, in a Portsmouth coffee shop, a local woman asked Hillary how she managed "to get out the door every day." The woman was actually interested in Hillary's ev-eryday beauty routines ("Who does your hair?" she went on to ask), but Clinton, after acknowledging that she had help with the hair, got serious. "It's not easy," she said, "and I couldn't do it if I didn't passionately believe it was the right thing to do . . . I just don't want to see us fall backward as a nation. This is very personal for me. Not just political." Clinton's eyes filled with tears. Widely televised, it indeed seemed to many viewers to be a moment when the personal and the political were fused, wrenchingly, in the experience of this woman.

When Clinton went on to win the New Hampshire pri-mary, many commentators attributed the win to those two moments. "Clinton has found her groove," said Richard Cohen of RealClearPolitics, while the wave that Obama had been riding finally "broke on the shoals of his cold indifference" and Hillary's "warm tears." I read that comment not for its accuracy (in his eight years as president, Obama was any-thing but "cold" or "indifferent"), but for what it says about men, women, and gender—for that reporter at least, Clinton had finally (it is implied) found the natural "groove" for a woman: "warm tears." Obama's corresponding failure was to exhibit the worst of masculinity: coldness. The up-and-coming rock star, once you removed the veneer of amiability, was still a man—and one who could hurt a woman—and the extraordinarily competent, poised, female candidate was actually a woman: vulnerable, open, warm, and hurting.

Of course, if Hillary had not merely teared up but actually begun to sob, the media reaction might have been very different. If her standard mode in debates and public appearances was the girlish vulnerability she displayed the night of the last debate, it's doubtful she would have been taken very seriously as a candidate. It's a difficult tightrope to walk, this business of projecting the right degree of feminine vulnerability, "softness," and "accessibility," while still appearing competent and strong. In an interview with *Humans of New York*, Hillary spoke of confronting that double bind when she was harassed by young men at the law school admissions test:

> I couldn't afford to get distracted because I didn't want to mess up the test. So I just kept looking down, hoping that the proctor would walk in the room. I know that I can be perceived as aloof or cold or unemotional. But I had to learn as a young woman to control my emotions. And that's a hard path to walk. Because you need to protect yourself, you need to keep steady, but at the same time you don't want to seem "walled off."

This is the classic dilemma of the "public" woman, and it's both age old and very current. Step outside the boundaries of appropriately contained feminine behavior and you are

likely to be perceived as unstable, shrill, overly aggressive, or
overly emotional. But being too controlled is a problem, too;
you then become "cold" and "stiff" and "unable to connect."
(Chuck Todd actually criticized Clinton for being "over-prepared" for her first debate against Trump.) You may be seen
as repellently "masculine." Golda Meir was called "the only
man in the cabinet"; Angela Merkel "the iron Frau"; Elizabeth
I of England spent her entire reign trying to walk a tightrope
between showing her subjects she had the steely "heart and
stomach of a King" while earning their love as the nurturing
mother of England. Hillary, of course, has had the continuing
problem with being "unlikeable" and fake, the polish and poise
she has had to develop in order to be taken seriously viewed as
a sign of insincerity and "inauthenticity," proof that she was an
ambitious, opportunistic politician who would craft her public
self as required.

Nearly all women, I suspect, have experienced some form
of the double bind that I've described. Hillary managed
to avoid it for longer than most. In college at Wellesley, she
was highly engaged in politics, respected by classmates as a
campus activist, and seen as "a sophisticated coalition builder
who provided extremely strong and very sensible leadership."
As a senior in 1968, she became the first student to address the
graduating class at commencement. She was just twenty-one
years old, headed for Yale Law School, and so politically passionate and self-assured that she dared to criticize the "empty
rhetoric" of the U.S. Senator who was the honored speaker.
Taking the stage after him, she boldly went off script:

"What does it mean," she asked of his speech, "to hear that
13.3 percent of the people in this country are below the

poverty line? That's a percentage." She and her classmates, Rodham says, demand "a more immediate, ecstatic, and penetrating mode of living"—a society 'where you don't see people as 'percentage points,' a restored "mutuality of respect."

That ideology was evocative of the 1962 Port Huron Statement and other "New Left" manifestoes that called for political action that was also a form of community building, and that would transform personal relationships and "consciousness" as well as institutions. In those days, such manifestoes were almost always delivered by male politicos like Tom Hayden (the principal author of Port Huron). Having a young woman present these views—and as a spontaneous criticism of the invited male speaker—was newsworthy. The speech was published in *Life*, and Hillary was interviewed by *The New York Times*. She was so politically engaged, so good at organizing and mediating, and so inspiring, that friends expected her to one day run for public office. Some even suspected she might make it to the highest office in the land: "A lot of us thought Hillary would be the first woman president," says Wellesley friend Karen Williamson. "I thought if ever in my lifetime there is a woman president, it would be her."

Today, we call that particular achievement "breaking the glass ceiling"—as though it represents the final frontier of equality. But in the sixties we were just getting into the wagons, and the terrain was rocky. It took an extremely well-balanced young woman like Hillary not to be thrown off. She was unusual in that she managed to remain committed to both her personal ambition and meaningful political work without (seemingly) undergoing the typical crisis of confidence that girls go through when romance enters the picture. It took years for Bill Clinton to convince her to live with him in Arkansas, and even longer for her to accept his marriage proposal. Through those years she continued to work for social change: with Marian Wright Edelman at the Children's Defense Fund, as a staff member on the impeachment committee investigating Nixon, as a university instructor in law, as director of a legal aid clinic, as a member of a prestigious law firm. And while I, seeing it as part of the romance of marriage, gave up "Klein" in exchange for "Bordo," Hillary already had a public life as "Rodham" that she wasn't keen to trade in for "Clinton." Bill was supportive. While others pressured her to change her last name, Bill "didn't ask me or even talk to me about my name." As she recalls in *Living History*, "He said my name was my business, and he didn't think his political future depended on it one way or another."

The fact that others did think Hillary's last name was a big deal, however, reveals a lot about the cultural context that Hillary and I share. As Gay White, the widow of Frank White (who ran in 1980 against then-incumbent Bill Clinton) recalls, "I cannot tell you the number of times [prospective voters] would say to me 'If your husband wins, are you going to keep his last name?' I heard it over and over and over." Hillary had never changed her name, and the people of Arkansans saw this as a rejection of the role she was supposed to adopt as first lady, not to mention wife. Bill was already seen as young and arrogant, and many believed his "radical feminist" wife contributed to his loss to White in that election.

"How they perceived her," says Gay White, "was very much a factor."

So she straightened her hair, got rid of her owlish glasses, put on some makeup, and changed her name. And Bill won the next time he ran.

It's easy, in 2016, to be scornful of these concessions. "If you think Hillary is so radical," said one Sanders supporter, "Why don't you ask her why she took her husband's last name when his political career took off?... Or why she played the adoring, skirt-suited wife while allowing him to put his career first?" But when Hillary and I were in high school, girls weren't even allowed to wear pants. And it wasn't very many years ago (and may be happening still in some places) that black women with naturals and corn rows were told by employers to go home and fix their hair. When I was about to go on the market for my first job, I was advised on how to style my hair so it would look less countercultural. At tenure time, the fact that I wore a tattered, *Flashdance*-style skirt then in fashion was actually raised as an argument against my promotion. A bit later, I lost a prestigious job because, as I was told by a confidante, I "waved my hands around too much" when I gave my job talk. Over time, I learned that to get my most important priorities successfully launched, I had to stop dressing like a D. H. Lawrence heroine and contain some of the impulses of my more spontaneous, "authentic" self.

The name change and the hair were Hillary's first concessions to the demands of having a public profile—demands that are very different for women and men, both physically and emotionally. While male politicians can relax with a pretty standard professional dress code and are rarely criticized for being too "serious," gruff, or "ungracious," women have to calibrate their outfits carefully to avoid being both too schoolmarmish and too sexually provocative, and to regulate their emotional presence to be both warm and charming *and* "tough enough to handle the job."[3] It goes from the (seemingly) trivial (fashion) to training in emotional composure. As Pat Schroeder, who explored a presidential run in 1987, remarked: if a man wants to look tough and industrious, all he has to do is "take off his tie, loosen his collar, roll up his shirtsleeves." But there's "no similar uniform for a woman. We tend to either look like unmade beds or look like a model." Bernie Sanders was not just permitted, but gloried in the scruffy, rolled-sleeves charm of the sixties male politico. Hillary, of course, was not allowed the same license to be bushy and unmanicured. Or grumpy. Even after she lost the election, she was expected to concede "graciously," and called a "sore loser" when she—justly—acknowledged Comey's interference. Sanders, on the other hand, looked like he was about to punch someone at the Democratic convention when Clinton officially got the nomination, and I never heard the word "ungracious" uttered by a single commentator.

Notions of acceptable public behavior, for men as well as women, have also changed dramatically over the years, and

---

[3] This double standard—only one of the many which dogged Hillary throughout both the primary and the general—is one teachers face as well. Female professors have seen it numerous times, reading student evaluations while serving on tenure and promotion committees: Males who hold to strict standards (of grading, comments on papers, etc.) are commended, while the female instructor who isn't "understanding" or "supportive" enough is described as cold and rigid. But then, female instructors who adopt more student-centered methods, who encourage the sharing of personal experiences, who have their students write journals rather than take tests, may be viewed as "touchy feely" and unprofessional.

vary depending on the culturally defined personae of the candidates. In 1992, wearing a pantsuit would have been a radical act for a first lady; in 2016, young women who identify as radical may see Hillary's pantsuits as symbols of her conventionality.[4] In 2012, Sarah Palin's poufy hairstyles, trim figure, and body-hugging skirts made her more attractively (and perhaps authentically) "feminine"; it wasn't the essence of her appeal to the GOP, but it unquestionably enhanced it. In 1992, all Hillary had to do was change her hairstyle and put on a pink suit and she was caricatured as pandering, twisting herself out of shape to gain acceptance. She wasn't expected to be feminine or glamorous, and on her pink seemed like a parody. When, in 1992, she defied the expectations of a first lady and took a very public role in championing health care reform, she was lambasted as ball busting, overly ambitious, power seeking. Yet because she stood behind her wayward man, as women are supposed to do, many young women nowadays see her as having condoned Bill's bad behavior.

The Perils of Female Ambition

The problem of the feminine double bind is compounded enormously for a woman like Hillary, who has been in the public eye for decades, trying to keep pace with changing expectations of feminine behavior while remaining true to herself. The press and public currently dislike Hillary for being guarded. But for Hillary, having a public life has involved

[4] The creation of "Pantsuit Nation" was a pro-Hillary appropriation of this, as hundreds of thousands of young women made the kind of outfit that they would normally not be caught dead in a symbol of support for Hillary.

hard lessons in the necessity of curbing unguarded, "spontaneous" reactions.

During Bill Clinton's campaign for President in 1992, the press
constantly compared Hillary to Barbara Bush, and the GOP re-
lentlessly accused her of threatening to "destroy the fabric of the
American family because she wasn't a stay-at-home mom," as
Tammy Vigie told *The Guardian*. Clinton defended her choices:
"I suppose I could have stayed home and baked cookies and had
teas, but what I decided to do was fulfill my profession, which I
entered before my husband was in public life."[5] The media was
all over it immediately, quoting, in a *Today Show* piece, women
who saw it as scornful of their own life choices—"She has no use
for us, we have no use for her," declared one—while neglecting
to include the rest of Clinton's remark. After "cookies and tea,"
Hillary had gone on to say, "the work that I have done as a professional, a public advocate, has been aimed . . . to assure that
women can make the choices, whether it's full-time career, full-
time motherhood, or some combination."

Quoting her remarks in full would have clarified Clinton's position. Instead of including it, the Today piece only mentioned
briefly that Clinton later apologized to stay-at-home moms, but,
as she notes in *Living History*, "the damage had been done." As
indeed it had. The GOP immediately labeled her a "militant feminist lawyer" and "the ideological leader of a Clinton-Clinton administration that would push a radical feminist agenda." Hostile
letters described her as "an insult to American motherhood."

Hillary suffered the consequences of another spontaneous

---

[5] Hillary's remark was actually not meant so much as a defense of her professional life as a response to Bill Clinton's opponent, Jerry Brown, who
had suggested that Bill was using his wife's connection with her law firm
opportunistically. That piece of the story was swallowed up, however, in
the gender flap that Hillary's comment generated.

remark later that same year when she was questioned about Bill's infidelity. Hillary had said she "wasn't sitting here, some little woman standing by her man like Tammy Wynette. I'm sitting here because I love and I respect him." Although the Wynette reference was to a famous song, not to Wynette herself, Tammy fired back: "I can assure you, in spite of your education, you will find me to be just as bright as yourself." Clinton's reaction—a slap on the forehead and rolling of her eyes—did not go over well. Nor did Bill's suggestion that he might make Hillary a member of his cabinet. Feminists like me were charmed by Bill's obvious admiration for his wife, but both he and Hillary were naïve in imagining that the mainstream reaction would be the same.

Earlier, while campaigning, Bill had (jokingly, according to Hillary) said their new slogan was "buy one, get one free." "Widely reported in the press," as Hillary recounts in *Living History*, the comment was then "disseminated everywhere as evidence of my alleged secret aspirations to become 'co-president' with my husband."

That year, Spy magazine ran a manipulated photo of Hillary Clinton as a dominatrix on the cover. Barbara Amiel of *Maclean's* wrote: "The first lady has emasculated America. I guess that is what radical feminists always wanted to do, but when the Bobbitt syndrome[6] hits the only superpower left in the world, it's not only the Mr. Bobbitts who are in pain. We all are."

The "Bill effect"—for good and for ill—has stayed with Hillary throughout her career. So long as the wives of famous men stay where they belong—in the background—they remain

---

[6] Lorena Bobbitt made worldwide headlines in 1993 when she cut off her husband John's penis with a knife while he was asleep in bed. At trial, she claimed that he had sexually abused and raped her. The penis, which she threw out of her car, was subsequently surgically reattached.

relatively untouched by their husbands' foibles. But from the beginning, "buy one, get one free" was never "free" for Hillary. The irony of Hillary's prominence as part of the Clinton power couple was that she paid for all Bill's mistakes while being minimized by his talents. So, on the one hand, if Bill gave a dazzling speech or charmed a group of voters at a diner, the press was sure to contrast it with Hillary's less-than-dynamic public speaking style or less-than-brilliant "retail politics." On the other hand, because Bill signed a racially problematic crime bill, or when he did something politically stupid during her campaigns, Hillary got dragged through the media muck with him.

The most bitterly ironic merging of the Clintons, one that fed mercilessly and unfairly into the "lying Hillary" caricature that became such a fixture of the 2016 campaign, resulted from Bill's evasiveness about Monica Lewinsky. Exploiting the ambiguity of our language (and attitudes) about sex, he denied (in testimony for the Paula Jones case) that he had had "sexual relations" with Monica Lewinsky, the twenty-two-year-old White House intern with whom he was sexually intimate—though short of intercourse.[7]

---

[7] The notion that oral sex doesn't constitute "real sex" isn't as unique as it was made out to be by Clinton's political enemies and the press. When I was a teenager (and perhaps among teenagers still, both straight and gay) actual intercourse was considered a defining dividing line. On one side, one was still just "fooling around"—and until you crossed over with someone, you were still a virgin. It's arguable, too, that Bill was being set up to lie, as David Brock suggests, and that the point of the Paula Jones sexual harassment case (which was ultimately dismissed as having no legal or factual merit) was precisely to "probe Clinton's consensual life through the deposition process, and then to question Clinton under oath about it."

Personally, I was less disgusted by Bill Clinton's attempts to avoid being exposed than I was by the probing into his and Monica's (consensual) sex life. But wherever your sympathies lay, it became clear, once the affair became an investigation of its own, that he was avoiding the facts (if not telling a lie) about his relationship with Lewinsky. Even worse (given his reputation as "slick Willy") was that he had done so in such a lawyerly manner, equivocating over words, always conscious of the need to keep his descriptions within what was "legal." Ultimately, when it was no longer possible to avoid it, he did admit to an "inappropriate relationship" with Lewinsky—at first tersely, and then in an orgy of apologies to everyone involved.

According to Hillary's own account in *Living History*, Bill's admission—which came a full seven months after the affair was leaked to the press—came as a devastating shock to her. Her quite intimate account reveals a marriage on the brink, and in writing about it, a women who was far from the "guarded" politician depicted by the right. Nonetheless, the cascade of concocted, hate-driven Clinton smear books that have appeared since then have portrayed the Lewinsky affair as involving a joint cover-up, in which Hillary lied as much as her husband. Worse than lied: enabled. In 2015, the "enabler" theory—studded with lies about how Hillary had personally tormented and bullied Lewinsky—was packaged and sold to young women in Katherine Timpf's *National Review* piece called "Hillary Clinton is Not a Feminist," and simultaneously perpetuated in countless stories and books, including Dinesh D'Souza's bestselling *Hillary's America*, which described Hillary as having "volcanic ambition" but being too "ugly, petulant and bitchy" to win a following of her own, and volunteering to serve as a front for Bill's "sex addiction" in exchange for entrance into the corridors of power.

"She would become his cover-up artist and his blame-the-victim specialist," D'Souza writes, "discrediting [women]'s allegations if they ever surfaced and protecting Bill from the consequences of his actions. . . . [J]ust as Hillary expected, Bill became fiercely attached—and hopelessly dependent on his enabler-in-chief." Such a florid fairy tale could be dismissed had it not become common lore among Hillary's political enemies and eventually made its way into mainstream media narratives.

I could fill this entire book with examples of the abuse, much of it powered by sexism, that Hillary has endured from the mass media—both right wing and, more recently, left leaning—over the course of her career. She has also had some all-too-fleeting periods when the popular press was sympathetic toward her. The highs and lows, however, have followed a familiar pattern: love her when she is down and/or graciously "serving" the nation; pull her down a peg or two (or twenty) when she gets too full of herself or aims too high. It's been an intense relationship that began decades ago, when as first lady she was deemed by conservative commentators as that most "unnatural" of creatures: an ambitious woman. She wanted an office in the West Wing! She tried to put through a plan for universal health care! She only had one child! She sneered (or so we were led to believe) at women who stayed home to bake cookies and serve tea. These crimes earned her epithets like "The Lady Macbeth of Little Rock" and "The Yuppie Wife From Hell"; a *New York Post* cartoon pictured Bill Clinton as a marionette, with a ferocious Hillary pulling the strings.

Hillary may not have always been seen as a spouse from

hell, but she has always stirred up the cultural unconscious—particularly around notions of what is expected and valued from women. It may come as a surprise to those more familiar only with the "untrustworthy," "corrupt" Hillary of the 2016 campaign that earlier attacks on her, besides those focused on her feminism and headbands, centered around what was seen as her ostentatious virtue and moral superiority. Rather than a tool of big money and establishment power, she was seen as overly zealous in her quest for moral justice and reform, and derided for "New Age" optimism.

When she gave a speech as first lady in 1993, arguing for "a new ethos of individual responsibility and caring . . . a society that fills us up again and makes us feel that we are part of something bigger than ourselves," columnists mocked her as an "aspiring philosopher queen." A *New York Times Magazine* cover story by Michael Kelly, called "Hillary Clinton and the Politics of Virtue," described her speech as "easy, moralistic preaching couched in the gauzy and gushy wrappings of New Age jargon." Inside the magazine, opposite the sarcastic headline "Saint Hillary," an illustration depicted the first lady beneath a golden halo.

Clinton the betrayed wife got more sympathy than "Lady MacBeth of Little Rock" or the "aspiring philosopher queen," but even then it was a mixed bag. *The Washington Times* editor Wesley Pruden actually sympathized with the women Bill Clinton was alleged to have had sex with: "He did Gennifer Flowers and Paula Jones, all right, but the devil in Miss Hillary made him do that . . . Maybe Hillary's long-suffering husband deserves not censure but a night out." Then, rather than quietly "stand by her man," she chastised the GOP, claiming the fevered investigation into Bill's extramarital blow jobs with Monica Lewinsky was part of a "vast right-wing conspiracy." As it turns out, she was right,[8] but the press didn't like either the conspiracy theory or the audacity of what was presented as an attempt to deflect from the "real"

---

[8] At the time, Hillary was denounced as being paranoid.

In 2017, things look a bit different. Arguably, the right-wing assault began in 1994, when the *Spectator* magazine launched the "Arkansas Project," assigning its reporters stories designed to ferret out any and all of Bill's or Hillary's activities that could be blown into "scandals." The magazine's key strategy, according to David Brock (who ought to know, as a reformed hit man for the magazine), was to turn the usurper Clintons into "metaphors for all of the social changes of the past thirty years that the right-wing base in the country hated": gay and women's liberation, draft dodging, sexual promiscuity, communism, and "diversity, multiculturalism, and political correctness."

Ultimately, this informally waged culture war became a more tightly orchestrated affair when Bob Dole, Newt Gingrich and other Republicans began calling for the appointment of an independent counsel to conduct a special investigation into "Whitewater" (one of the many overbloated "scandals" that ultimately showed no wrongdoing on the part of the Clintons.) The first appointee as OIC, Robert Fiske, issued no indictments, which displeased the Republican Right. This led to the engineering of Fiske's replacement by Kenneth Starr, a rabid conservative with (as we were to find out) a taste for dirty details, who was determined to keep the investigation going as long as possible, but who by the fourth year, to his consternation, had turned up nothing. Frustrated, Starr requested and received permission from Attorney General Janet Reno to expand his investigation beyond Whitewater to "look into possible criminal charges against the President." The possible criminal activity involved Bill Clinton's word-parsing testimony before a civil case that was totally unrelated to Whitewater (Paula Jones's charges of harassment), but the investigation that followed unleashed all of Starr's pent-up fury at Clinton. Whitewater, "Travelgate," and "Filegate" had all produced nothing. This new one—officially an investigation into Clinton on charges of perjury and obstruction of justice, but in practice a sordid, sleazy excuse to probe and publicize his extramarital relationship with Monica Lewinsky—paid off big time. The pattern—one investigation leading to another and another, until some kind of pay dirt is unearthed—has continued with the GOP's investigation into Benghazi, out of which came the "email scandal."

story: Bill's equivocating on the word "sex." Still, when the Clintons left the White House, Hillary had been battered and bruised enough to earn the right to run for senator of New York State, an office in which her productive but low-key performance earned her praise.

It was only when she—oops—started "leaning in" again (Facebook chief operating officer Sheryl Sandberg's phrase for women pushing against the professional limits placed on them) and dared to try for the presidency, that the "hellish housewife" (as Leon Wieseltier called her) was reincarnated, this time without the "housewife" part.

"The second she becomes partisan and political," one of her 2008 campaign advisors said, "she becomes a little bit more radioactive." Not surprisingly, the right flank led the charge: Hillary was "satan" (Don Imus), "Mommie Dearest," "the debate dominatrix," and "Mistress Hillary" (Maureen Dowd). But it wasn't just right-wing journalists and pundits. Hillary, in seeking more power, stirred something up among her fellow Democrats, too. "Power-seeking men," as one Harvard study found, "are seen as strong and competent. Power-seeking women are greeted by both sexes with 'moral outrage.'" Left-leaning politicos were hardly exempt from demonnizing metaphors and imagery. MSNBC's Chris Matthews, an ardent Obama supporter, described Hillary as a creature from the bowels of hell: "witchy" and a "she-devil."

For a woman, the opposite of "leaning in" is graciously "serving," whether cookies and tea or as a junior senator who underplayed her celebrity and deferred to those with seniority (Carl Bernstein even referred to her performance in the Senate as "deferential"). Even the GOP seemed to like Hillary when she was doing that. When she left the Senate, she was commended by politicians on both sides of the aisle for her compassionate service to New York during 9/11 and her ability to work with Republicans as well as Democrats. As Secretary of State, she served President Obama (to whom, let's not forget, she lost her first presidential run) so dutifully, was such an exemplary public servant and team player, that she she left office with a 69 percent approval rating—"remarkably high numbers," Nate Silver noted, "in an era when many public officials are distrusted or disliked." Hillary had worked extremely hard to rebuild America's public image abroad, with great success. She also developed, during that time, an enduringly close relationship with Obama. When she fell and suffered a concussion, Obama was both concerned and solicitous. When he asked Clinton's secretary, Capricia Marshall, at the annual holiday party which Hillary was forced to miss, "How's my girl doing?" he went on to tell Marshall "I love her, love her, I love my friend."

By 2014, a year before Hillary announced her intention to run for president, a *Times*/CBS News poll found that 82 percent of Democrats favored Clinton over both Joe Biden and Elizabeth Warren, and a Quinnipiac poll reported that registered voters in Ohio (yes—Ohio) chose Clinton over the six likely Republican candidates: Jeb Bush, Marco Rubio, Rand Paul, Ted Cruz, and John Kasich. "If the election were held tomorrow," John McCain said, "Hillary Clinton would most likely be the President."

But as her friend, and former congresswoman, Ellen Tauscher had warned her before she left the State department, that would all change once she actually entered the ring. "The moment you move back into politics," Tauscher had said, "you go from 66 to 46 to 26 faster than a split second." In April of 2015, Hillary announced her candidacy, and within weeks, John McCain's prediction was replaced (by the press) with her annoying "presumption of inevitability," and her GOP colleagues began to alchemize everything good that she had accomplished while serving her country, transforming the gold into ashes. Her tenure as secretary of state became "Benghazi" and then "the email scandals." Her years of experience trying to find common ground in a highly polarized government became evidence of her enmeshment in "establishment politics." Her ability to moderate between progressive goals and the necessities of working within a consumer capitalist society (yes, like it or not, that is what we are) became "being in the pocket of Wall Street." And every time she tried to explain—anything—she was branded as "lying," "deflecting," or "covering up."

It was relentless—and if you think this is an exaggeration, just take a look at the June report from Harvard's Shorenstein Center which showed that even when "scandals" were not involved, 84 percent of Clinton's coverage was negative compared to 43 percent of Trump's and 17 percent of Sanders's. The report notes: "Clinton's negative coverage can be equated to millions of dollars in attack ads, with her on the receiving end."

It's no wonder that Hillary, as she describes it, learned to "think before I speak" and "sometimes sound careful with my words. [It's] not that I'm hiding something, it's just that I'm careful with my words." The irony is that this caution engendered an abiding, low-level hostility toward her from the media. We saw this frequently during the election cycle—in complaints about her lack of press conferences, the constant descriptions of her "secretive" and "calculating" responses to the press, and the snide side comments about her "carefully choreographed appearances" and "halting" answers. The construction of this cagey Hillary Clinton was so relentless, so embedded in virtually every story about her, that it made no difference whether you were watching Fox News or MSNBC—unlikeable, untrustworthy, unpopular Hillary was all you were going to get.

When I discussed this with my students, one of them remarked, "It sounds like Hillary was damned no matter what she did. She was so competent and so experienced! So smart! What kind of women would Americans find acceptable for president?" It was a good question, and one which I've often pondered, noting how many other countries seem to be more comfortable with women leaders that are forceful and don't particularly project the vulnerability and softness that we still associate with "femininity."

For a time during the primary, Bernie Sanders supporters were fond of saying, "I'd love a woman for president, just not this one. If Elizabeth Warren were running, she'd have my vote in a minute." But when Elizabeth Warren was actually running for the Massachusetts Senate, she had to deal with charges of being "harsh" and "unlikeable." Other women were "turned off" by Warren's "know-it-all style," and she was charged, like Clinton, with "inauthenticity." "I want her to sound like a human being," said a Democratic analyst for Boston radio station WBUR, "not read the script that makes her sound like some angry, hectoring schoolmarm."

How would Warren's political passion play if she were actually a candidate for president? I can already see the words "strident" and "shrill" in an imaginary news report. I often wonder, too, whether it wasn't precisely Hillary's self-knowledge, steadiness, and composure—the very qualities that made her success possible—that also set her up for the vicious backlash that she has had to endure.

2.

The "Woman Card" Moves to the Bottom of the Deck

On the evening of the 2012 election, CNN published a post-mortem on "where the GOP went wrong." The headline read: "How Women Ruled the 2012 Election." Pointing to the 11 percent advantage Obama held over Romney with women and the record number of Senate seats won by women, reporter Halimah Abdullah remarked, "In many ways, the 2012 election was the year of the woman."

It's hard to believe this was only four years ago, and it's startling to review the differences between what seemed to matter then as opposed to in the 2016 contest.

The fact is, 2012 was a year in which a fairly innocuous gaffe by Mitt Romney about how he looked for female cabinet prospects by examining "binders full of women" launched hundreds of comedic parodies, outraged protests, social media rants, and a devastating rejoinder by Obama ("I've got to tell you, we don't have to collect a bunch of binders to find qualified, talented, driven young women") that made women fall even more in love with him than they already were. Described in 2013 as "the gaffe that will never die," many commentators believed at the time of the election that Romney never fully recovered from the "binders full of women" remark.

But 2016? That was the year in which GOP contender

Donald Trump could routinely insult women's bodies, brag about grabbing them by the genitals, have twelve women come forward to accuse him of sexual assault, and have it all evaporate—poof!—by Election Day.

The election of 2012 was marked by heated controversies over reproductive rights, beginning in February with a partisan showdown over a federal mandate requiring religiously affiliated institutions (such as universities and hospitals) to offer coverage for contraceptives to employees. When Georgetown law student Sandra Fluke testified for the Democrats, describing the economic hardship that paying for contraceptives caused students and low-income hospital staff, Rush Limbaugh called her a "slut" and a "prostitute" who is "having so much sex she can't afford the contraception." Limbaugh's remarks set off a firestorm of support for Fluke, and Limbaugh was eventually forced to apologize for his "insulting word choices" that had created such a "national stir."

The "national stir" was far from over, however. Throughout the election season, conservative politicians, weighing in on the abortion debate, learned that words really do matter—or at least, they used to. In August, Representative Todd Akin, Senate candidate from Missouri, arguing against exceptions for rape victims, said that in instances of "legitimate rape," women rarely get pregnant: "The female body has ways to try to shut that whole thing down." He was defeated in the election. In October, Senate candidate from Indiana Richard Mourdock said during a debate that "Life is a gift from God. And, I think, even in the situation of rape, that it is something that God intended to happen." He was defeated in the election. The same month, vice presidential candidate Paul

Ryan gave an interview in which, defending his position that there should be no excuses for abortion, referred to rape as a "method of conception." His career survived, and indeed thrives, but he was still forced to explain that he wasn't advocating rape as a fertility aid.

These comments might have had little impact had the national press and mainstream media not headlined them—and the issues they brought to the surface—on front pages and television programs, going so far as to raise the specter of a GOP "war on women."

In 2016, in contrast, vice presidential candidate Mike Pence's career militating against Planned Parenthood and federal funding for pregnant victims of rape barely generated mention in the papers or political news shows. Nor did his 2014 bill requiring that all women seeking an abortion have an ultrasound eighteen hours before the procedure and that all fetal remains from abortions and miscarriages be buried or cremated. Given this lack of attention from the press, I wonder how many female millennials who viewed Clinton and Trump presidencies as equally repellant realized that if Mike Pence had his way, they would be holding funerals for any fetuses they aborted or miscarried?

As for our president, who knows what he really thinks about reproductive issues? He used to be "in a meek fashion pro-choice," as he told Bill O'Reilly in March 2016, but would now "protect the sanctity of life in the biggest way" he can, by stocking the Supreme Court with pro-life judges. Indeed, he had become so "pro-life" that, pressured the same month by MSNBC host Chris Matthews to give a yes or no answer to the question of whether or not there should be punishment for abortions, he replied that "the answer is . . . there has to

be some form of punishment." (You could see the gears turning in his brain, as he tried to figure, obviously for the first
time, what the right answer was in this new quiz show). "For
the woman?" Matthews asked, knowing he had hit pundit's
pay dirt but wanting to make sure it was clear to viewers, to
which Trump replied, "Yes." Trump later walked back his
remarks, in a statement in which he said that doctors who
perform the services are the ones who should be punished.
But when, after the election, *60 Minutes* correspondent Leslie
Stahl questioned him about the consequences of a repeal of
Roe v. Wade, he waved aside the issue of the effects on women
living in states that would outlaw legal abortions: "They'll
have to go to another state," he shrugged, as though describing a minor inconvenience (which I suppose it is if you have a
private jet).

In 2012, the notion that women who get abortions should
be punished or Pence's proposal for fetal funerals would have
ranked, along with Akin's and Mourdock's remarks, as monumental misogynist mistakes, politically speaking. In 2016,
they slid off the candidates into a growing heap of "gaffes"
that the press largely ignored.

What had happened in the intervening years?

It certainly wasn't the case that conservative Republicans quit their efforts to institute state control over wom-
en's bodies—if anything, they doubled down. In June of 2013,
Texas Republicans attempted to pass an "omnibus" bill that
would criminalize abortion after twenty weeks and impose
such harsh restrictions on abortion clinics that 90 percent of
them would be forced to shut down. (That was when Senator Wendy Davis led a thirteen-hour filibuster to delay a vote
until after the midnight voting deadline and became an in-

stant feminist hero.) Then 2014 kicked off with Mike Huck-
abee describing pro-choice Democrats as "patronizing"
women by treating them as though "they cannot control their
libido or their reproductive system without the help of the
government." Throughout that year, conservative legislatures
in many states passed a slew of restrictions aimed at making
abortion inaccessible, even if technically legal under Roe v.
Wade. It was, indeed, a "banner year for anti-abortion laws,"
in which Paul Ryan led the charge with a "conscience clause"
in the appropriations package that would allow employers to
refuse to cover contraception in their health insurance plans
for moral reasons. The Republican National Committee even
delayed its annual winter conference so that members could
attend the annual March for Life, an anti-abortion rally in
Washington, D.C.

But 2014 was also a year in which ISIS, a militant group
that few Americans had heard of before, began a series of
beheadings that brought the threat of terrorism to the front
page once again—a prominence that continued into 2015, with
the attack on French satirical magazine *Charlie Hebdo*. Fur-
thermore, 2014 was the year of the Ebola epidemic, and the
year when the killings of unarmed Eric Garner and Michael
Brown gave rise to protests, and Ferguson, Missouri, rightly
dominated domestic news as a national debate began over
police violence, racial bias, and the criminal justice system
that virtually never indicts the officers involved. By 2015,
Black Lives Matter was far more pressing a political movement than the battle over choice—which had, after all, been
going on for years, and usually behind the doors of legislative
buildings rather than in the streets of major cities. The far
more newsworthy "gender issues" involved transsexual and

gay rights—and when, in June of 2015, the Supreme Court ruled that same-sex marriage was a constitutional right, many Americans may have believed, either with dismay and anger or joy and relief—that we were on a progressive path as far as gender was concerned. Economic and racial inequality, on the other hand, seemed to have been left behind by the Left—and were now claiming their due.

Despite the racial and international turbulence, the presence of the Obamas in the White House—while infuriating to white supremacists and a political annoyance to the GOP—was deceptively comforting to those of us who cared passionately about social justice issues, women's equality included. THIS IS WHAT A FEMINIST LOOKS LIKE: Obama proudly held the T-shirt in front of him, and we knew it wasn't pandering. It was real. You only had to look at and listen to Michelle Obama—or see pictures of Barack and Michelle together, and with their daughters—to know that. With the Obamas in charge, with reproductive rights still secure for the economically privileged, with the right to marry whomever you loved, and (seemingly) a new cultural permission to be whatever sex (or combination, or none at all) you felt yourself to be, it was easy for younger women in particular to imagine that the gender wars were over, and that those who persisted in foregrounding "women's issues" were a victimizing relic of the past. Hannah Weinberger, in a CNN piece about the state of millennial feminism, quoted a twenty-four year old: "Women think we all need to look out for each other, and that ends up shooting us in the foot because then we're thought of as incapable. If a woman stood up for herself as a person (instead of) demanding rights based on gender, I think that'd be a much stronger platform."

Disdain for Feminist "Political Correctness" Unites the Right and the Left

Skip now to April 25, 2016, the day before the Pennsylvania primaries. This was the day that Trump appeared on *Fox & Friends* and introduced the term "Crooked Hillary" ("because she's crooked," he helpfully explained). He also declared, in the same interview, "The only thing she's got is the woman card." What he meant, of course, was that Hillary was running as a sort of affirmative-action hire, exploiting her gender to remind "politically correct" liberals that it was time, after all these years, for a female president. The notion that we are all hog-tied and tongue-tied by oppressive lefty notions about what's "correct" had been a feature of conservative arguments since the so-called "culture wars" of the 1990s, in which feminists and others were charged with "closing the American mind" (Allan Bloom) and destroying higher education (Dinesh D'Souza). Trump wasn't the first to use it in political campaigning, but he certainly had the biggest megaphone for it.

Trump supporters adored his attacks on "political correctness," whether he aimed them at the Democrats' "pandering" (as he described it) to racial and religious inclusiveness or to feminist sensitivities. "I know I'm not supposed to say this," he'd often begin, and then go on to say it anyway, to thunderous shouts of appreciation from his audience. Commentators may speculate about whether his comments incited racism, sexism, homophobia, and Islam-

ophobia, but one thing seems sure: whatever form his tirades against "political correctness" took, they released the
Freudian id—permission to behave "badly," to cut the apron
strings, to defy the schoolmarm, to say "fuck you" to the re-
pressive do-gooders—among his followers. Be as bad as you
want; your new Papa Trump says it's ok.

Factually, the notion that Clinton—probably the most experienced, qualified person to ever run for president—was
campaigning only "on her gender," is ridiculous. But that
notion wasn't held by Trump alone—or even primarily by
Republicans. Younger feminists, who didn't like being pi-
geonholed by their gender or by language, had for some
time been expressing frustration with what they saw as the
ideological rigidity of their mother's generation of feminists.
"I'm not interested in playing language police," said Erin
Matson, action vice president for NOW in 2013. "If someone says to me, 'I'm really pissed about what they're doing to
birth control right now in Congress, but I don't know if I'd
call myself a feminist,' I don't really care."

I agree with Erin Matson that it's more important to
fight for reproductive rights than to fuss over the title of
"feminist." At the same time, I doubt that Matson would
be happy to find that in 2016 her frustration with the "language police" aligned her—at least on that issue—with
Donald Trump. Matson was trying to define her own form
of feminist politics; Trump has no use for *any* form of feminist politics. Big difference. Yet there was an overlap there,
and it crystallized around the notion that Hillary Clinton
was "playing the woman card." When I published a pro-Hillary piece in February 2016, that's how it was taken by many
readers, even though there was nothing in my piece to suggest anyone should vote for Hillary "because she's a woman."

These were some of the comments:

> Frankly, I find nothing more irritating than the concept that it is "time" for a woman in the White House, or that somehow it is Hillary's "turn" to be president. I would love to see a woman in the White House, but it has to be the right woman, and frankly, gender, race, religion, or any other such characteristic should not be the reason one votes for a candidate.

> Do we want a woman president? Of course we do. But we only want the right one—and that right one is not Hillary. Voting for her because she is a woman—which she reminds us of, ad nauseam, is . . . sexist.

> It is ridiculously sexist to vote for Hillary because she's a woman. That is a tactic the Republicans tried and thankfully failed at in 2008.

Bernie Sanders fans, in particular, were always ready to pounce with their own variant of Trump's charge that Hillary was playing "the woman card." They took Madeleine Albright (the first female secretary of state) to task early in the primaries when, during a Clinton rally in New Hampshire, she said that electing the first female commander in chief would be a true revolution, and that "there's a special place in hell for women who don't help other women."

That line, which Albright had been trotting out at women's conventions since 2006, was such an old feminist chestnut that it had been memorialized on Starbucks's coffee cups. But if you didn't know the history behind it, and didn't realize it was a quotation—rather than a pronouncement specially formulated for the non-Hillary supporter—you could easily take it as a nasty slam. And Sanders supporters did. They interpreted it as "telling them how to vote" and suggesting they weren't good feminists for supporting a man. "Shame on . . . Madeleine Albright for implying that we as women should be voting for a candidate based solely on gender," *The New York Times* quoted twenty-three-year-old Sanders supporter Zoe Trimboli as saying.

Albright wasn't implying any such thing. Her "true revolution" remark was a (justified) jab at Sanders, who had been claiming sole ownership of revolutionary politics, and the "special place in hell" quote in a room full of Clinton supporters was pretty much equivalent to quoting "Happiness is a warm puppy" at a Humane Society rally. But in an article titled "Gloria Steinem and Madeleine Albright Rebuke Young Women Backing Bernie Sanders," that context was lost. In the same article, the *Times* invoked a (imagined, anonymous) gender-obsessed feminist to contrast against "young women who would like to see a female president elected someday" but "do not necessarily want to base their vote on that single factor."

Sanders himself tacitly endorsed these critiques of "the woman card," "doubling down," as Katha Pollitt noted, on the "idiotic quip by his surrogate Killer Mike ('A uterus doesn't qualify you to be president of the United States') with the pseudo-lefty pledge: 'No-one has ever heard me say, "Hey guys, let's stand together, vote for a man." I would never do that, never have.'" And, as I mentioned earlier, at a post-election book tour stop—but still apparently running against Clinton—he made his disdain for what he called "identity politics" very clear.

The fact is, I have yet to meet the Clinton supporter whose support was based on the "single factor" of her gender. At the same time, it's striking to me how effectively this election cycle managed to silence any excitement over the possibility of electing a woman. Why were we bullied into suppressing these feelings? It certainly hadn't happened when we celebrated the first black president; African Americans refused to be cowed into hiding their delight over Barack Obama. As the mother of a teenager who is both black and female, I want her world to be one in which we recognize the struggles and achievements of both identities without being accused of playing a "card."

When Trump accused her of playing the "woman card," I would have liked Hillary to do a version of Reagan's wryly weary "there you go again"[9] with respect to such deliberate distortions of her candidacy. Or, perhaps to remind voters that just because there wasn't a label for it, that didn't mean the "man card" wasn't being played every hour of every day, in contests over the size of hands as surrogate penises (Marco Rubio: "Have you seen his hands? And you know what they say about men with small hands"), who had the most "stamina" and "strength," and even—in the *Access Hollywood* tapes— who could get away with the most groping of women.

It was cruder than usual in 2016, but displays of masculinity are traditional features of elections—Bush in his shirt-sleeves working around his ranch, Reagan on his horse—and "softness" is always suspect. Bill Clinton was derided for being weak (like a woman), and teased about his appetite for

[9] In the 1980 debate with Jimmy Carter, this was Reagan's response to Carter's accusation that Reagan wanted to eliminate Medicare. Reagan's "There you go again," which he said with a chuckle, is frequently cited as among the most effective debate one-liners of all time.

junk food and natural tendency to chunkiness. Thank goodness Obama could make up for his embarrassing performance
bowling with his prowess on the basketball court. Even Bernie
Sanders got into it with Trump, when he appeared on Seth
Meyers and dared Trump to match his "toughness" against
his own, after describing a week of "knocking his brains out"
campaigning in California.

It would have done my heart good to see Hillary deconstruct
the whole idea of the "woman card" in some way. Instead, the
day after Trump accused her of having nothing going for her
but the fact of her gender, Hillary responded: "The other day,
Mr. Trump accused me of playing the, quote, 'woman card.'
Well, if fighting for women's health care and paid family leave
and equal pay for women is playing the woman card, then deal
me in!" Within days, plastic "woman cards" were being sold
on Hillary campaign sites, and Clinton had begun to use "deal
me in!" as a signature tag line at her campaign speeches—so
often that even I (who was one of the first to order the plastic
card) would wince as I felt it coming. *No, Hillary, please don't
say it again,* I'd pray silently.

Hillary wasn't wrong to try to change the terms of the
dispute from running "on gender" to being an advocate for
women's issues. And if Donald Trump had been her only challenge, owning "the woman's card" on her own terms might
have been sufficient, for there were many moments when
women, even GOP women, were forced to recognize that
gender equality was hardly a done deal. The same evening
Hillary asked to be "dealt in," Trump repeated and embel-
lished what he said on *Fox & Friends*, claiming that if Hillary
were a man "I don't think she would get 5 percent of the vote.

The only thing she's got going is the women's card. And the beautiful thing is, women don't like her." In the background, but visible to the cameras, Chris Christie's unfailingly smiley wife Mary Pat rolled her eyes and seemed to grimace. It was one of the few spontaneous moments during GOP events when something like female solidarity interrupted partisan politics. Criticizing Hillary for exploiting "political correctness" by "playing the woman card" was one thing, apparently; every Republican could get behind that. Turning Hillary into the high school mean girl was another—at least, for Mary Pat.

GOP women hadn't been pleased, either, when, in September 2015, an article appeared in *Rolling Stone* describing Trump's reaction, while watching the news on his lavish private jet, to a shot of candidate Carly Fiorina.

"Look at that face!" he muttered in disgust and disbelief. "Would anyone vote for that? Can you imagine that, the face of our next President?! I mean, she's a woman, and I'm not supposed to say bad things, but really folks, come on. Are we serious?" During the second Republican debate, Jake Tapper asked Fiorina to comment. Looking very much the steely nerved businesswoman, Fiorina replied, "I think women all over the country heard very clearly what Mr. Trump said," and the room burst into applause. Nasty remarks about women's appearances—as the revelation of Trump's behavior toward beauty queen Alicia Machado later showed—evoke an immediate sense of sisterly identification, memories of personal hurt, anger at the double standard of a world in which women are judged for the slenderness of their legs or the smoothness of their skin; but overweight, aging celebrities like Trump can (as Trump himself claimed in the *Access Hollywood* tapes) "do anything they want" to any woman they want.

Trump might well have been taken down by "women's

issues"—his poll numbers were falling steeply after the release of the *Access Hollywood* tapes—had James Comey not
reminded the nation that a secretary of state's use of a private
email server was far more serious than a would-be POTUS's
pussy grabbing. I'll discuss that in a later chapter. For now,
I note that the "woman card" was already severely rent—
among the Democrats themselves—by the time Trump discarded it entirely. While Democratic women had felt united
and empowered in 2012, protesting in unison against clueless
Republican misogynists who didn't know the first thing about
women's bodies, in 2016 they were divided—by generation.

3.

Bernie Sanders
and the "Millennials"

Feminist Generation Gap

Many books have been written about the way racial differences among feminists both divided and pushed feminist thinking and practice forward over the past several decades. In the 2016 election, however, it was not race but generation that was the dynamic factor among left-leaning women. Women like me, who experienced many cultural battles in the "gender wars" firsthand—from the first scornful comments that journalists had heaped on "women's libbers," to the public shaming of Anita Hill, to the renewed threats to bodily rights that we thought we had won decades earlier—brought to the 2016 campaign a personal knowledge of the fragility of feminist accomplishments and an identification with Hillary that was deeper and longer than any current headlines. We may have winced—as I did—when Albright quoted a coffee-cup version of feminism or Hillary said "deal me in." But we understood that behind every seeming appeal to "sisterhood" was the history of what was indeed a revolution—and one that was far from over. We knew the role Hillary had played in that revolution, and the price she had paid for it. Many of us, too, had followed Clinton through the course of her public career, had read her autobiography, and knew very well that the accusation that she had come to issues concerning racial and economic justice "late" and "for political purposes" was among the most extraordinary fabrications of the campaign.

Many younger women, on the other hand—no less feminist, no less committed to gender equality—had formed their ideas about "The Clintons," as Savannah Barker reminds us, in the shadow of twenty years of relentless personal and political attacks. Few of them—as I know from decades of teaching courses on feminism, gender issues, and the social movements of the sixties—were aware of the "living history" (to borrow Hillary's phrase) that shaped the woman herself. These young women weren't around when the GOP, appalled that "liberals" like the Clintons had somehow grabbed political power, began a series of witch hunts that have never ended. (Hillary was correct: it has been a "vast right-wing conspiracy," from the *Spectator* magazine's "Arkansas Project," designed specifically to take Bill Clinton down, to Kenneth Starr's relentless digging into Bill's private life, to the Benghazi and email investigations.) They hadn't experienced a decade of "culture wars" in which feminists' efforts to bring histories of gender and race struggle into the educational curriculum were reduced to a species of "political correctness." They didn't witness the complicated story of how the 1994 crime bill came to be passed or the origins of the "super-predator" label (not coined by Hillary and not referring to black youth, but rather to powerful, older drug dealers).

It isn't necessary, of course, to have firsthand knowledge of history in order to have an informed idea of events and issues. When it came to Hillary Clinton, however, sorting out fact from politically motivated fiction was a difficult task, particularly if one's knowledge was filtered through the medium of election-year battles. The 2016 election was no academically rigorous history course; it was dominated by versions of "Hillary Clinton" constructed by her political opponents and transmitted by reporters who usually don't see offering context as their job and don't have the time (or, for some, the inclination) to sort fact from fiction. And then, too, after decades of harsh schooling in the ways of politics and the media, Hillary herself was no longer the outspoken feminist who chastised reporters when they questioned her life choices, but a cautious campaigner who measured her words with care. I knew just what one of my graduate students meant when I asked her how "millennial" feminists saw Hillary and she said, "a white lady." A white woman herself, she wasn't referring to the color of Hillary's skin, or even her racial politics, but rather what was perceived as her membership in the "dominant class," all cleaned up and normalized, aligned with establishment power rather than the forces of resistance, and stylistically coded (her tightly coiffed hair; her neat, boring pantsuits; her circumspection) with her membership in that class. When I looked at Hillary, I saw someone very different—but I understood the basis for my student's perception.

Any rift between feminist generations, however, would almost certainly have been healed by Trump's outrageous comments and behavior, had younger progressives not become bonded, during the primary, to a Democratic male hero who both supported the issues they were most passionate about, and offered young women independence from the stale and, in their view, defunct feminist past. These young women weren't going to rush to order a plastic "woman card" for a candidate that had been portrayed by their hero as a hack of the "establishment." They didn't believe in "sisterhood"—a relic of a time when, as they had been told (often in women's studies courses), privileged, white feminists clasped hands in imagined gender solidarity, ignoring racial injustice and the problems of the "working class." They didn't want to be dealt any cards at a bridge game organized by Gloria Steinem or Madeleine Albright—or Hillary Clinton. They wanted Bernie Sanders.

Sanders Brands Hillary as "Establishment"

Before I go any further, let me put my own cards on the table. The destruction of Hillary Clinton, I firmly believe, while propelled by a "perfect storm" of sexism, partisan politics, and media madness, was bookended by two immensely powerful assaults. One was the inappropriate, inaccurate, and inflammatory interference in the general election by FBI director James Comey, which I'll discuss in a later chapter. The other occurred much earlier, during the primaries, but its consequences are felt even today. I know I will make some of my younger feminist colleagues (and other left leaners) furious, which was distressing to me then, and still is. These people, in so many ways, are my "natural" colleagues, and most are as upset as I am by Trump's victory. But they played a big role in the thin edge (not a landslide, as Trump would have us believe) that gave Trump the election. For while Trump supporters hooted and cheered for their candidate, forgiving him every lie, every crime, every bit of disgusting behavior, too many young Democrats made it very clear (in newspaper and Internet interviews, in polls, and in the mainstream media) that they were only voting for Hillary Clinton as "the lesser of two evils," "holding their noses," tears still streaming down their faces over the primary defeat of the person they felt truly deserved their votes. Some didn't vote at all. And as much as I am in agreement with many of his ideas, Bernie Sanders splintered and ultimately sabotaged the Democratic party—not because he chose to run against Hillary Clinton, but because of *how* he ran against her.

Sanders often boasted about the importance of "the issues" rather than "individuals," of not playing dirty politics or running nasty ads in his campaign. And it's certainly true that he didn't slime Hillary by bringing Bill's sexual accusers forward or by recommending that she be put in jail, as Trump did. He also seemed, at the beginning of the primary season, to be refreshingly dismissive about the "email scandal": "Enough already about the damned emails!" he shouted at the first debate, and I remember thinking "Good man, Bernie! Way to go!" But within months, taking advantage of justified frustration with "politics as usual" (a frustration more appropriately aimed at GOP stonewalling of Democratic legislation), Sanders was taking Hillary down in a different way: as an "establishment" tool and creature of Wall Street.

"I think, frankly," he said in January, campaigning in New Hampshire, "it's hard to be a real progressive and to take on the establishment in a way that I think [it] has to be taken on, when you come as dependent as she has through her super PAC and in other ways on Wall Street and drug-company money."

Progressive. It's a term with a long, twisty history. In the nineteenth century, it was associated with those who argued for the moral "cleansing" of the nation. A century ago, both racist Southern Democrats and the founders of the NAACP claimed it for their purposes. The Communist Party has described itself as "progressive." By the time Sanders argued that Clinton was "not a true progressive," the word was not very useful descriptively—one can be progressive in some ways and not so progressive in others, and no politician that I know of has ever struck every "progressive" chord. Context matters, too. As Jonathan Cohn wrote, in May: "If Sanders is the standard by which you're going to decide whether a politician is a progressive, then almost nobody from the Democratic Party would qualify. Take Sanders out of the equation, and suddenly Clinton looks an awful lot like a mainstream progressive."

For Sanders supporters, however, "progressive" wasn't an ill-defined, historically malleable label, but rather a badge of honor, a magical talisman for those who considered themselves "anti-establishment." It may have been "a fallback identifier for pretty much anyone *The Nation* and its journalistic kin smiled upon" (as Michael Kazin described it), but it was an identifier with a great deal of potency, particularly for a younger generation longing for lives organized around something other than job hunting. When Sanders denied that badge of honor to Clinton he wasn't distinguishing his agenda from hers (their positions on most issues were, in reality, pretty similar), he was excluding her from the company of the good and pure—and in the process, limiting what counted as "progressive" causes, too. His list didn't include the struggle for reproductive rights or affordable child care. Nor, at the beginning of his campaign, was there much emphasis on racial justice.

As I watched Sanders enchant the crowds, it was something of a déjà vu experience to see a charismatic male politician on stage telling women which issues are and aren't "progressive." Cultural histories of the sixties rarely acknowledge what a sexist decade it was. We imagine that breaking through the suburban fifties fantasy meant that old-fashioned gender roles and attitudes had been discarded. Far from it.

In fact, in many ways the decade was more male-centric than the fifties; it just privileged a different sort of male. Those men loved having us as uninhibited sexual partners and helpers in their political protests, but they never let us forget who was in charge of creating the platforms or who belonged in the political spotlight. Working in the South for voting rights, young activists like Casey Hayden and Mary King[10] had gained sophisticated organizing experience and found strong female role models they could respect in the older black women who were such a central part of the civil rights movement. But by the mid-sixties, as Black National-ism, the "student movement," and anti-war protests moved to the center of cultural prominence, white activist women found themselves both unwelcome within black identity poli-tics and demoted within the other movements. Charged with making coffee while the male politicos speechified, shouted down and humiliated for daring to bring up the issue of gender inequality during rallies and leftist gatherings, their early calls for sexual equality were seen as trivial, hormonally inspired, and "counter-revolutionary." Inspired by the Black Panthers to look to their own oppression, women began to speak up about what came to be known as "personal politics." But unlike the Panthers, women were told over and over that they had to subordinate their demands to "larger" causes in the interests of "the movement." They found themselves sim-

[10] Hayden and King were members of the Student Non-Violent Coordinat-ing Committee (SNCC) who wrote a famous "memo" that became a found-ing document of the emerging Women's Liberation Movement.

mering and stewing as boyfriends and husbands defined what
was revolutionary, what was worthy, and what was "progressive."

It was both an exhilarating and a frustrating time to be
an activist woman. Some, like me, dropped out of the fight
for a time. Others became more violently countercultural and
joined the Weather Underground. Others still became leaders
of the emerging women's movement. In 2016, however, many
activists saw that movement as part of "establishment" politics and no longer requiring their revolutionary fervor. As one
Sanders supporter wrote:

> Yes, equal rights for women and minorities are critically
> important. To consider these ideals progressive, however,
> seems passé. At this point, it's more fair to suggest they
> are traditional. Gender and civil rights and equality may
> remain under attack from the right, but these ideals are
> positively engrained in two generations of Americans.
> Progressive voters, at this stage in our young country's
> political history, want to challenge corrupt systems. The
> prison-industrial complex, the military-industrial com-
> plex, the financial-industrial complex, and the other lob-
> bies that control our politicans and our government, for
> example.

I'm fairly certain that Sanders himself doesn't see "equal
rights for women and minorities" as so firmly inscribed in our
culture as to be "traditional" or "passé." Nonetheless, Sanders
gave Clinton no credit for her long-standing progressivism
in these areas, while identifying her with the corruption he
was dedicated to cleaning up. Organizing against the abuses

that he made his signature causes was indeed a worthy progressive agenda. Portraying Clinton as the enemy of systemic change, on the other hand, was not only factually incorrect, but proved politically disastrous in the general election.

Sanders was the perfect vehicle to revive political passion both among the older left, revitalized by being on the side of "the revolution" again, and a younger generation who had yet to experience the sense of "rightness," community, and belief in the possibility of radical change that nourished us in the sixties. Here was this guy who had lived through it all, who looked like a grandfather but spoke like a union organizer, who was making it seem possible again—but in terms that spoke to the present, to their issues. He was fierce, he was uncompromising, and he wasn't afraid to call out clear enemies, which revolutions always need to rally around. Wall Street. Greed. Big Money. Super PACS. The "Establishment."

Initially, I liked Bernie Sanders a lot, and identified with him. In terms of class, geography, and religion, I actually have much more in common with him than I do with Hillary Clinton, whose background was solidly middle class, Methodist, and Midwestern. Sanders and I share the same immigrant, working-class Jewish roots. The neighborhood he grew up in in Brooklyn looked very much like the one I'd grown up in in Newark, New Jersey. Although Sanders was a few years older than me, we had belonged to the same left-wing groups— Sanders while in college, I while in high school. We even went to the same college—University of Chicago—and I sometimes wondered whether I'd seen him on campus when I was a freshman and he a senior. As his campaign took off, and despite my support for Hillary, it made me smile to hear someone who sounded like he could have been a relative deliver speeches to mass audiences.

Sanders's branding of Hillary as "establishment," however, seemed vastly unjust and corrosively divisive to me, especially when delivered to a generation that knew very little about her beyond what Bernie told them. Like *progressive, establishment* is a pretty meaningless term, particularly when lobbed at one Washington politician by another. Neither Sanders nor Clinton had been working "outside the system." Appearances to the contrary, Sanders was not a union organizer, but rather a longtime member of the Senate. And if Clinton had more support from the Democratic Party, that was due in large part to the relationships she had cultivated over the years, working with others—something Sanders was not particularly good at.

Nonetheless, for weeks during the early months of the primary, I listened to nineteen-year-olds and media pundits alike lavish praise on Bernie Sanders for his bold, revolutionary message, and scorn Hillary for being a part of the "establishment." They described him as "heart" and her as "head"—a bitter irony for those of us familiar with the long history of philosophical, religious, and medical diatribes disqualifying women from leadership positions on the basis of our less-disciplined emotions. He was seen as "authentic" in his progressivism while she was pushed to the left by political expediency—as though a lifetime of fighting for equality, and children's rights meant nothing. He was the champion of the "working class" (conveniently ignoring that black and white women were members, and that their issues were also "working class" issues), but her longstanding commitments to universal health care, child care, paid sick leave, racial justice, the repeal of the Hyde Amendment, and narrowing the wage gap between working men and women apparently evaporated because she'd accepted well-paid invitations to speak at Gold-man Sachs.

Later, the news media even let Sanders get away with de-scribing Planned Parenthood and NARAL as "establishment" when he didn't get their endorsement. They made little of it when he described abortion as a "social issue" (as though loss of control over one's reproductive life has no impact on one's economic survival). They accepted, without question, his de-scriptions of himself as an activist for feminist causes, when all he had done was vote the right way in the Senate. They posted pictures of him being arrested at a protest against the University of Chicago's real estate investments, while making no mention of the work Hillary had done, when she was the same age, investigating racist housing practices with Marian Wright Edelman. Clinton's emails and her "trust problems" were the only stories about her they were interested in re-porting.

"I didn't recognize the Hillary they described"

In February 2016, at the Iowa caucus, Clinton described her-self as "a progressive that likes to get things done" and was loudly booed by a robust Sanders contingent in the audience. The Hillary Clinton that I had been following for decades—who had spent her entire public life promoting, yes, progres-sive issues—was clearly not registering with these booing Sanders supporters. So I typed up a blog for *Huffington Post*. I began by saying, "I am one of those 'over 65' women who belong to the faceless, aging 'demographic' with a Hillary sign on my front lawn," and went on to describe my frustration with the way Hillary was being imagined, recalled the sexism prevalent during the political movements of the sixties, and reminded those who had booed Hillary of her lifelong commitments.

I wasn't expecting the piece to hit such a live nerve, both among Clinton and Sanders supporters. The former showered the piece with thousands of "likes" and the latter with a torrent of hate mail for me, Hillary, and my generation of feminists. I was startled by how few Sanders supporters understood that the piece was addressed to those who had booed Hillary, not to Sanders supporters in general, and that I wasn't telling anyone who to vote for but protesting what seemed to me an unwarranted hostility toward Clinton. I didn't recognize the person they seemed to be addressing as me, any more than I recognized the Hillary Clinton they described:

> I am a woman and a feminist and I will not be taken in by the identity politics that Hillary and her supporters are using to install her in the White House. Her decisions are her own and she should be judged by them. It's not sexism to hold her to the high standards we should require from someone to put into the highest office of our country. She chose to enrich herself from the very corporations and people who have captured the government and she is not immune because of her gender.

> Hillary Clinton is the worst enemy to women. She bullies victims of a serial predator, and her policies are toxic to the most vulnerable women.

> Sorry that younger folks don't embrace your "woman-at-all-costs" brand of feminism.

Hillary doesn't just have ties to the establishment, Hillary is the establishment.

A real feminist doesn't need to sell her soul and her entire country along with it just to get ahead. Hillary will do whatever it takes to get the power she thinks she deserves. It has all to do with her last name and nothing to do with feminism.

I'm not interested in the woman who won't take a stand on something until it is politically correct/safe to do so. I'm not interested in the woman who is a career politician clearly out of a desire for power and wealth and ego. I'm interested in the candidate who has been quietly doing the right thing before Hillary even decided she was going to run someday for president.

From what I know, second wave feminism has mostly been the purview of privileged white ladies like you, like Hilary. Has it occurred to you that while you accuse us of not knowing history, you're frozen in it, trying to score that one big victory by getting one of your own in office? Meanwhile, us third-wavers are concerned with class gaps, race issues, and LGBT issues, too.

The argument that [Hillary] was ever a leading feminist is just silly, she never was. She was a "one note nancy" who began her own political career while serving as first lady. She used Health Care to launch her political career, it was safe to do as the wife of a very popular President.

Comments like these (even more than what had made me write the piece in the first place) made me aware of the enormous gap between my understanding of Hillary Clinton and the privileged, inauthentic, and cynically political "establishment" creature that Sanders supporters booed in Iowa.

What fertile generational soil Sanders had mined into! As early as 2008, younger women were describing Hillary less as the feminist warrior and more like a club member of an older, more "conventional" generation. In a book that came out that year called *Thirty Ways of Looking at Hillary*, Amy Wilentz writes: "Most of the time, she looks like a Republican. She gives off something between a country-club, golf-playing, hedge-funding vibe, with a whiff of bingo games, Sunday church-going, supermarket aisles and coffee klatches."

"I have yet to meet a woman who likes Hillary Clinton," contributes Katie Roiphe. "She is trying too hard, and the spectacle of all this trying is uncomfortable, embarrassing. One could feel in a palpable way the smart woman's impersonation of the pretty woman, the career woman's impersonation of the stay-at-home mom; one could feel a lack of grace." Ariel Levy chimed in that Hillary's speeches had become "cloying and generic." (Even Rebecca Traister, who eventually was to become a supporter of Hillary, was a "young Hillary hater," who in early pieces compared her to Darth Vader—"more machine than woman, her humanity ever-more shrouded by Dark Side gadgetry.")

When *Thirty Ways of Looking at Hillary* was written there was as yet no email scandal, no Clinton Foundation flap, no Benghazi, no Wall Street speeches, no controversial trade deals, and no revelations of earlier comments about "super predators." There was no particular policy reason for feminists to find Hillary so cringeworthy. It seemed, rather, that she had begun to remind them of their mothers. As I discovered when I looked up the ages of these writers, Hillary could well have been the mother of Roiphe or Levy, born in 1968 and 1974 respectively (Wilentz in 1959). Strikingly, the most sympathetic pieces in the volume come from Katha Pollitt and Deborah Tannen, both born in the 1940s. Pollitt and Tannen undoubtedly had been faced with similar dilemmas to those that faced Hillary; I know I have.

"When women talk, some people think we're shouting"

At times during the Sanders/Clinton primary campaigns, the double standard did get some attention. Sanders was a habitual bellower at his rallies. But pundits didn't go "ouch" about his speaking voice, the way they did with Clinton. ("Why is she so shrill? Why doesn't she modulate? Doesn't she realize she has a microphone?") Jay Newton Small, in *Time*, suggests it's because men's shouting is seen as political passion, but when women raise their voices the specter of a punishing mommy rises up. It unpleasantly evokes personal memories of being scolded because we were "in trouble," and makes us want to run away.

At the October 16 Democratic debate, after Clinton accused Sanders of voting with the gun lobby, Sanders had replied, "All the shouting in the world is not going to do what I would hope all of us want, [which] is keep guns out of the hands of people who should not have those guns." Clinton's response then, which she had tried out at several smaller events and then repeated on October 23 in a speech to the Democratic National Committee Women's Leadership Forum, was: "You know, I've been told to stop, and I quote, 'shouting' about gun control. It's just that when women talk some people think we're shouting."

The audience cheered and hooted, and Clinton went on: "I will not be silenced, because we will not be silenced."

It was clearly not fair to Sanders, who had been using the term "shouting" in lots of speeches not about Clinton, but rather as shorthand for "making a big deal over," and he protested: "I certainly do not have a problem with women speaking out—and I think what the secretary is doing here is taking words and misapplying them." But fair or not to Sanders, it was certainly true of the pundits' nasty cracks about Clinton's voice. Bob Woodward, on *Morning Joe*, suggested she "get off this screaming stuff." Joe Scarborough, who had been interviewing him, agreed: "Has nobody told her the microphone works?"

The complaints about Clinton's "screaming" had a resonance beyond voice, though. There are some barbs that appear to transcend political and generational divides between women: Being told to "simmer down" when we are angry. Being accused of "making too much of a fuss" about something we take seriously. Being expected to "play nice," to be sweet and obliging. When Hillary put the "When Women Talk Some People Think We're Shouting" quote up on her Facebook page and campaign website under the headline, "Hillary Clinton Just Said Something Women Have Been Thinking for Years," she was calling out a truth that clicked with many women, and it went way beyond complaints about the decibel level of women's voices. It went to the experience of being made to feel too demanding, too pushy, too whining, too angry, too ambitious, too aggressive, too greedy, too bossy, too argumentative when aski5 ng for or doing exactly the same thing as a man would be applauded for.

Around the same time, actress Jennifer Lawrence wrote a piece in Lena Dunham's *Lenny* saying she, too, was fed up and "over trying to find the 'adorable' way to state my opinion and still be likeable." The turning point for her was when she gave her opinion about the disparity between her salary and her male co-stars in a "clear and no-bullshit" way; no aggression, just blunt," and the man she was working with acting as if she had been yelling at him. "All I hear and see all day are men speaking their opinions, and I give mine in the same exact manner, and you would have thought I had said something offensive . . . Fuck that. I don't think I've ever worked for a man in charge who spent time contemplating what angle he should use to have his voice heard. It's just heard."

Women of all ages "got it."

Sanders doubles down . . .and his supporters follow

When the "shouting" incident occurred, some reporters predicted it was the first shot in a "gender war" in which Clinton would have the upper hand. But that never happened. Many Sanders supporters, ignoring the evidence of history, still pronounced him "more of a feminist" than Clinton. (In fact, Katha Pollitt had it exactly right: "Bernie is a traditional leftist for whom feminism is a distraction.") And as her primary victory became inevitable, Sanders himself seemed to abandon any scruples he may have had against describing Clinton as the handmaiden of the devil. An interview with George Stephanopoulos on May 23, 2016 contained this exchange:

SANDERS: We need a campaign—an election—coming up which does not have two candidates who are really very, very strongly disliked. I don't wanna see the American people voting for the lesser of two evils. I want the

American people to be voting for a vision of economic justice, of environmental justice, of racial justice. That is the campaign we are running, and that's why we are getting the support we are.

STEPHANAPOLOUS: Is that how you would describe Hillary Clinton against Donald Trump—as the lesser of two evils?

SANDERS: Well if you look—No, I wouldn't describe it, but that's what the American people are saying.

It was very Trump-like of Sanders to get his digs in by referring to "what people are saying." But, like Trump, he got the message through loud and clear. A month earlier, in April, Hillary had held between 71 and 82 percent of Sanders's supporters; by the beginning of June that number was between 55 and 72 percent. He made no attempt to correct "Bernie or Busters" when they said things like: "If we don't get Bernie, we're not just going to automatically vote for the demon." Nor did he dispute Susan Sarandon when she described Hillary Clinton as "more dangerous" than Donald Trump.

No, Sanders never said to "lock her up." But as the primary election made way for the general, he made no attempt to disentangle Hillary Clinton from the DNC "rigging" his surrogates and campaign manager constantly complained about—a "myth," according to Kurt Eichenwald, that vastly overestimated the power of the DNC and portrayed the party as a "monolith that orchestrated the nomination of Hillary Clinton against the will of 'the people.'"

First, it was the number of debates, presented as a conspiracy against Sanders. In fact, the number initially proposed—six—was exactly the same number proposed in 2012.

Then it was the primaries that were closed to independents—surely not inappropriate considering they were Democratic primaries, and conveniently ignoring the huge boost Sanders got from caucuses, which favored young, healthy, economically privileged students who could spend hours hanging out at them without having to worry about child care or money lost from time off from work.

Finally, it was the Russian hack of DNC emails that "'proved' the organization had its thumb on the scale for Clinton." As Eichenwald points out, those emails were almost all from May 2016, at which point Sanders had no hope of winning the nomination, except through a massive "flip" of superdelegates—a rather odd strategy for someone running a campaign in the name of "the people." Yet he was still hammering away at Clinton, invoking the words "Goldman" and "Sachs" as often as possible, and delivering crowd-pleasing sarcasm about Clinton's unreleased transcripts of her speeches. Ignoring that the fees, outrageous as they are, are standard (if not on the low side) for famous folk, he used the line, over and over: "It must be a fantastic speech, a brilliant speech which you would want to share with the American people. It must be Shakespearean!" As to the DNC emails, as Sanders himself later admitted, we surely would have found emails just as nasty, if not worse, had Sanders's campaign been hacked as well.

Did Sanders have every right to continue his campaign? Yes. Did he do serious damage to Clinton's chances of winning over Trump every time "devil" and "demon" were used to describe her and he offered no protest, every time he portrayed her as the servant of Wall Street whose impending victory was stolen from "the people" by a "corrupt" DNC? Again, yes. Undoubtedly yes.

As the Democratic National Convention approached, "Bernie or Busters" began to organize protests. The first night of the convention was disrupted by anti-Hillary hecklers in Bernie shirts handing out posters that said "War Hawk" and "Goldman Girl" and "Monsanto Mama" on them. "You can't expose the corruption of the political system and then expect us to get behind the same political system," said one of the organizers, in a CNN piece in early June. "If Bernie Sanders does not walk out of that thing as the nominee, we can guarantee you from that point on we'll start the de-registration of the Democratic Party." Reading these comments, I couldn't help but think back to 2008, and my own very different reaction to Obama's primary win. I had been a strong Hillary supporter, and also a bit suspicious of Obama, who initially seemed too young and too slick to me. But he had impressed me enormously with his "race speech," and although the primary with Hillary had gotten nasty at times, neither he nor she had ever led me to believe that the other was the "enemy." As a Democrat, my overriding concern was the general election and defeating the GOP. Hillary was my choice, but I never considered not getting behind Obama with everything I had to give, and I've never regretted it.

In 2008, Clinton had helped her supporters get there, too. Like Bernie, she ran until the bitter end. But four days after the voting ended, she got out of the race and endorsed Obama passionately:

The way to continue our fight now, to accomplish the goals for which we stand, is to take our energy, our passion, our strength, and do all we can to help elect Barack Obama, the next president of the United States. Today, as I suspend my campaign, I congratulate him on the victory he has won and the extraordinary race he has run. I endorse him and throw my full support behind him. And I ask all of you to join me in working as hard for Barack Obama as you have for me.

Clinton's unqualified endorsement of Obama was an immeasurable help in uniting the party. In contrast, weeks after Clinton had officially secured the majority of pledged delegates (on June 7), Sanders was still delivering his stump speech, broadcast on national television, saying his "political revolution" was just beginning, while Clinton supporters waited in vain for his endorsement. There had been rumors that it would be coming on June 17, but they proved wrong. The speech designated for that day was highly anticipated— and bitterly disappointing to Clinton supporters. "The major political task that we face in the next five months," he said, "is to make certain that Donald Trump is defeated and defeated badly." But he then went on to repeat his critiques of economic, racial, and environmental inequalities in the country. Strikingly absent was an endorsement of Clinton. Instead, he emphasized "the *significant* difference between him and Hillary on *VERY, VERY* important issues" (emphasis Bernie's) and called on his supporters to continue his "revolution": "We need new blood in the political process, and you are that new blood."

Those of us expecting an endorsement were not only angry, but insulted. Many of us considered ourselves political progressives, yet to Sanders we were apparently just old, stale blood, clogging the veins of the revolution, agents of a corrupt "establishment." And when he spoke of taking the party back for "working people" and young people and out of the hands of rich donors, I wondered—not for the first time—how the hundreds of thousands of African Americans who supported Clinton fit in. Did he think they all owned Bentleys or were simply too old to matter?

Bernie's core supporters, of course, were right there with him that night, many "gathered at Bernie-watching parties, like one in the East Village of Manhattan, where twenty supporters in the upstairs dining room of the Bareburger restaurant broke into raucous applause when he said his twelve million votes proved that his was not a radical campaign, but rather 'mainstream.'" Yamiche Alcindor of *The New York Times* reported that Jessica Stokey, forty-three, a television editor, was one of many who shed tears: "I don't know if it's just my imagination, but it looked to me like the bags under his eyes got bigger and his face grew more thin," she said. "That's when I started crying. It's like knowing the zombies are here and you have to save your child; that's how heartbreaking it is," she added. Other supporters who had gathered for his speech, when asked about Clinton, replied that "she doesn't speak for me or my issues." In the days that followed, those who had come around to accepting the fact that she was the nominee invariably prefaced their reluctant support with phrases like "I don't really like Mrs. Clinton, but . . ." And too many remained who were actually hoping Trump would win: "[He's] an asshole," said one, "but I feel like he's full of hot air. HRC is calculating, she's conniving . . . If [she] wins in November, I feel like she will do whatever she can to squash the progressive movement. That movement dies." Some, like Susan Sarandon, believed that a Trump win would help make "the revolution" happen quicker—the old lefty theory that exposing the contradictions and abuses of capitalism was a prerequisite to the system collapsing under the weight of worker uprising.

Among the most unjust consequences of Sanders's branding Clinton as an establishment tool was the effect on young African Americans. Their parents—particularly their mothers—were virtually solid in their support for Clinton, and that wasn't the result of her racial "pandering" (as Trump later suggested) but rather Hillary's quiet, steady work, over decades, on issues of "kitchen-table" importance to black families and the relationships she had built with black leaders. That history was either unknown to or ignored by many Sanders supporters; Clinton "has to be willing to get out of what's comfortable and get on the streets," said one, obviously ignorant of the fact that at the age of twenty-four, Hillary had been a civil rights activist who went undercover to investigate discrimination in public schools. Hillary was also the first candidate to pay attention to the Flint, Michigan, water crisis, joining forces with Flint's mayor long before Bernie showed up in town. But like Clinton's work on LGBTQ issues, decades old rather than campaign inspired, none of this made it into flashy stories headlining her lifelong commitment to racial, gender, and sexual justice. Instead, we were treated to a huge media flap over a mistake she made, misdescribing Nancy Reagan as fighting for AIDS research (when it was quite the opposite). Sanders made sure that "1994 Crime Bill" and "super-predator" defined Clinton on racial issues, especially for those active in the Black Lives Matter movement, who were influential in shaping the perceptions of other young black Americans.

In fact, Sanders himself, along with many black leaders, had voted for the crime bill—which many later regretted, Clinton included. (Hillary was first lady at the time, and didn't have a vote—although she vocally supported the bill.) She also apologized profusely for using the "super-predator" label, even though in her speech it was not aimed at African American youth but the dealers who exploited them. (I strongly suspect "predator," for child-advocate Clinton, was less inflected racially than with connotations of child abuse.) But for too many millennials, both black and white, "1994 Crime Bill" and "super-predator" said all one needed to know about Clinton. Some spoke as though she was personally responsible for the spike in mass incarceration that was a consequence of her husband's bill. "She was part of the whole problem that started sending blacks to jail," a young black man from Ohio observed. He wasn't alone. Another—a millennial black woman, also from Ohio, likened the choice between Clinton and Trump to the choice "between being stabbed and being shot." Sports icon Colin Kaepernick, famous for kneeling during the national anthem as a form of protest, described both Trump and Clinton as "evil": "Both are proven liars and it almost seems like they're trying to debate who's less racist."

In the meantime, in June and early July, a GOP united against Clinton (if not yet happy with Trump) was pushing hard on the email "scandal" that Sanders had once so gallantly dismissed. But Sanders was no longer offering his "enough with the damn emails" position, allowing Republicans and James Comey to dish the dirt without interference. When he finally endorsed Hillary on July 12, speaking to a crowd in which many of his supporters jeered her name and held signs saying "Won't Vote Hillary," he looked grumpy and grudging and devoted most of his speech to congratulating himself and his followers on the "fight to create a government which represents all of us, and not just the one percent—a government based on the principles of economic, social, racial, and environmental justice." He boasted of the races he had won, and was unable to resist a jab at party leaders by citing Clinton's abundance of superdelegates (read, in

Sanders's code: party hacks). He conceded that she "will be the Democratic nominee for president," and then went on to formally endorse Hillary Clinton—finally.

It was not exactly a rousing call, designed to energize his supporters and redirect their passion toward Clinton. While Clinton had focused her endorsement for Obama on his accomplishments and abilities, Sanders returned once again to his own campaign, citing the impressive attendance at his rallies, and emphasizing that "this campaign is not really about Hillary Clinton, or Donald Trump, or Bernie Sanders, or any other candidate who sought the presidency. This campaign is about the needs of the American people and addressing the very serious crises that we face." Conceding that "as we head into November, Hillary Clinton is far and away the best candidate to do that," he then launched into what was essentially an accounting of the economic and social positions he and Hillary shared, which gave the lie to the vast gulf between "revolutionary" Bernie and "establishment" Hillary that he had run on.

Of Hillary's qualifications to run the nation, Sanders mentioned just two accomplishments: "as a great first lady who broke precedent in terms of the role that a first lady was supposed to play as she helped lead the fight for universal health care" and "as a fierce advocate for the rights of children." Stellar accomplishments, yes, but rather gender typed, and hardly doing justice to the myriad ways in which Clinton had served the country.

Bernie may have been feeling his age that day. If so, I sympathize. But when my tattered memory fails me, I look things up. During the second GOP debate, Carly Fiorina had issued the absurd challenge: "If you want to stump a Democrat, ask them to name an accomplishment of Mrs. Clinton's." Here's what those who wanted to know would have found out (I'll leave out Hillary's Wellesley and law school accomplishments, and the trade deals that one wouldn't expect Sanders to regard as accomplishments):

- Co-founded Arkansas Advocates for Children and Families
- Staff attorney for Children's Defense Fund
- Former director of the Arkansas Legal Aid Clinic
- First female chair of the Legal Services Corporation
- Twice listed by the National Law Journal as one of the hundred most influential lawyers in America
- Worked to keep minors out of prison in South Carolina
- Arkansas Woman of the Year in 1983
- Chair of the American Bar Association's Commission on Women in the Profession
- Created Arkansas's Home Instruction Program for Preschool Youth
- Led a task force that reformed Arkansas's education system
- Instrumental in passage of the State Children's Health Insurance Program
- Promoted nationwide immunization against childhood illnesses
- Successfully sought to increase research funding for prostate cancer and childhood asthma at the National Institutes of Health
- Worked to investigate reports of an illness that affected veterans of the Gulf War (now recognized as Gulf War Syndrome)
- Helped create the Office on Violence Against Women at the Department of Justice

- Initiated and shepherded the Adoption and Safe Families Act
- Traveled to seventy-nine countries during time as FLOTUS
- Helped create Vital Voices, an international initiative to promote the participation of women in the political processes of their countries
- Helped create the Children's Insurance Program
- Delivered one of the most quoted human rights speeches of all time in Bejing, China
- Served on five Senate committees:
    Committee on Budget (2001–2002)
    Committee on Armed Services (2003–2009)
    Committee on Environment and Public Works
        (2001–2009)
    Committee on Health, Education, Labor and
        Pensions (2001–2009)
    Special Committee on Aging
- Member of the Commission on Security and Cooperation in Europe
- Instrumental in securing $21 billion in funding for the World Trade Center site's redevelopment
- Took a leading role in the investigation of health consequences of first responders and drafted the first bill to compensate and offer the health services our first responders deserve (Clinton's successor in the Senate, Kirsten Gillibrand, passed the bill)
- In the aftermath of 9/11, worked closely with her senior Senate counterpart from New York, Senator Charles Schumer, on securing $21.4 billion in funding for the World Trade Center redevelopment
- Proposed a revival of the New Deal–era Home Owners'

Loan Corporation to help homeowners refinance their
mortgages in the wake of the 2008 financial disaster

- Brokered a ceasefire between Hamas and Israel
- Brokered a human rights agreement with Burma
- Was the most traveled secretary of state to date
- The Clinton Foundation, founded by her and her husband,
  has improved the living conditions for nearly four
  hundred million people in over one hundred and eighty
  countries through its Initiative program
- Introduced the Family Entertainment Protection Act,
  intended to protect children from inappropriate content
  found in video games
- Former U.S. secretary of state
- As secretary of state, made LGBTQ rights a focus of
  foreign policy
- As secretary of state, worked aggressively on issue of
  climate change
- Grammy Award Winner
- Author

In all of this, Bernie Sanders found nothing around which to
rally his supporters.

4.

"Untrustworthy Hillary"

Hillary's "Health Scare"

In September, Hillary had pneumonia. Like many women, she carried on despite her doctor's advice. She insisted on attending a 9/11 commemorative ceremony and nearly fainted—something that has happened to others standing in the sun at long political events. (Obama has sometimes joked about it during his rallies: "Whoops, there goes another one.") Then she committed the sin of disappearing from the media's sight for ninety minutes, while she sought calm and cool—and water—in her daughter Chelsea's apartment.

The media immediately issued a missing person alert. Where was she? Where did she go? When a video surfaced showing her unsteadily entering her van supported by the secret service, and the news of her pneumonia was released, reporters were convinced she had been deliberately concealing her illness, revealing it only when she was "caught in the act" of fainting. When she emerged from Chelsea's apartment, she seemed smiling and well—another cause for suspicion. Was it really pneumonia? And if so, why hadn't she told the press about it? Hillary's explanation was that she didn't announce her illness because she thought she could just push through, no big deal. And as it turned out, John Kerry and others had also suffered pneumonia on the campaign trail without announcing it to the world. But this was Hillary Clinton, and every move was suspect. The mainstream media played and replayed the visual of her knees buckling, and relished in posing the "lingering questions" that remained concerning Hillary's "health scare." The campaign was being "tight-lipped," which only roused suspicions that more was going on than a case of pneumonia. "Opponents," wrote a team of NBC reporters, "are already seeing the incident as proof of their claims that Clinton has been hiding health issues."

The notion that Clinton was "covering up" more serious health issues was indeed a favorite among the right wing. "How sick is she?" Rush Limbaugh challenged, "and how much are they continuing to keep from us?" Helpfully filling in the details for those who had somehow avoided seeing the tape, he described her "head bobbing up and down as though she's having a seizure," people holding her up on each side, and a "near collapse" after which she is "shoved in the van" and taken to Chelsea's apartment. "The real question," he asked ominously, "is just how bad is it?"

The right-wing press proposed a number of answers. Perhaps the pneumonia story was a cover-up for Parkinson's disease, Cliff Kincaid intimated, noting that Clinton had been wearing blue-tinted sunglasses, which a medical website had suggested as an aid for Parkinson's patients. Others suggested she was hiding a traumatic brain injury that she had suffered during a long-ago fall, and there was much talk of "seizures" and "dysphasia" (a language disorder resulting from brain damage), descriptions of her as "exhausted" (or without "stamina," as Trump was fond of putting it) and unable to stand up on her own. There were constant demands for fuller health records from Clinton—while Trump produced a laughable doctor's letter describing his health in such rigorous medical language as "astonishingly excellent" and declaring that he would be "the healthiest individual ever elected to the presidency."

The most deadly charges against Clinton, however, was what the *Daily News*'s Gersh Kuntzman described in a piece headlined "Clinton's cover story for her pneumonia diagnosis further proves her first instinct is to lie":

"Hillary Clinton will beat pneumonia," Kuntzman wrote. "But she won't beat a condition far more fatal: untrustworthiness. In the hours after the Clinton campaign finally came clean (or did it?) . . . the larger question that will be raised by the "health scare" is the one that has dogged Clinton forever: Why does she create cover stories rather than reveal the truth?"

The pneumonia "health scare" (as it was called, though neither Hillary nor her doctor seemed scared at all) was just one episode in the neverending saga of "Untrustworthy Hillary." It goes back many years. "For decades," as Jill Abramson writes, Hillary has been portrayed as "a Lady Macbeth involved in nefarious plots, branded as a 'congenital liar' and accused of covering up her husband's misconduct, from Arkansas to Monica Lewinsky." But neither in Clinton's run for the Senate in 2000 nor in her presidential campaign in 2008 did the issue of "trust" play such a major role as it did in 2016. Hillary's main PR problem in 2008 was described more in terms of her "unlikeability," an issue that, as I described earlier, got Obama in some trouble during the final debate. It

wasn't until 2016 that the fiction of a perennially lying, calculating, untrustworthy politician emerged full force. Once
it did, it became fair game to slime her, to mock her, to call
her a bitch, a witch, a harlot—not because Hillary the woman
wasn't still there (for those who cared enough to look for her),
but because she had been replaced in the media by a fiction—a
fiction so powerful that Clinton could run against the biggest liar and most unscrupulous con man ever to appear on
the American political scene and still be seen as less "honest"
than him.

No, I'm not talking about "Fake News." For sure, we had
plenty of that, and consumers were often befuddled by Internet and social media disinformation that passed itself off as
reputable reporting: "Thousands of fraudulent ballots for Clinton uncovered." "Megyn Kelly fired after endorsing Clinton."
"Elizabeth Warren endorses Bernie Sanders." "The pope endorses Trump." "The Clintons bought a $200 million house in
the Maldives." "Hillary Clinton bought $137 million in illegal
arms." "Huma Abedin and Hillary longtime lesbian lovers."
"Hillary Loses Popular Vote by Several Million. Here's Why."
Such stories not only went viral, but sometimes crept into
mainstream publications. But focusing on Internet fakery, as
the mainstream media has been happy to do, conveniently lets
them off the hook for their own contribution to the fiction of
"untrustworthy Hillary." The distortions by reporters at such
reputable news sources as *The New York Times*, CNN, *USA
Today*, MSNBC, etc.—partly the result of unconscious gender
bias, some fueled by longstanding hostility toward Clinton,
and all motivated by the need to satisfy an audience habitu-
ated to consumable, easily digestible narratives and less and
less concerned with facts—played a far greater role in the disaster of the election than any Facebook story.

Is Hillary actually untrustworthy? The fact-checkers say, unequivocally, no. Indeed, she turns out to be the most truthful of all the candidates, her record for truth-telling better than that of Bernie Sanders, someone whom the press has never trashed for lying, even when he clearly was—about the circumstances of his visit to Rome,[11] for example. As for Trump: "If deception were a sport," writes Nicholas Kristof in *The New York Times*, "Trump would be an Olympic gold medalist; Clinton would be an honorable mention at her local Y." All politicians, of course, fudge stuff. Yet throughout the election, pundits could spend hours shaking their heads over what Joe Scarborough called Clinton's "mind-boggling lies" while treating Trump's stream of total fabrications—74 percent of his statements are lies, according to Politifact (Trump's description of Clinton as a "world-class liar" is a clear projection)—as business as usual.

It's kind of extraordinary, isn't it? And now that Trump is president, it's terrifying.

How did we let this happen?

---

[11] On April 8, Sanders's appearance with Joe and Mika on *Morning Joe* was highlighted by the "surprise" announcement that Sanders had been invited to Rome to give a "high-profile" speech on "the moral economy" at the Vatican. Both Sanders and his campaign manager Jeff Weaver suggested that the invitation had come from the Vatican itself and would include a meeting with Pope Francis. In fact, the invitation "to attend" (not present a speech) came from the Political Academy of Social Sciences—essentially an academic association—and it was only after the headlines had performed their own brand of persuasion (with some help, perhaps, from Sanders's pal in the Academy, Jeffrey Sachs) that the program was changed to list him as a speaker rather than—as he was originally listed—one of the "Other Participants." When he did meet the pope—very briefly and at the last minute—it seemed clear Francis was merely being polite in circumstances not of his own design.

Sexism Released

In the midst of the pneumonia hysteria, Stephen Colbert, addressing Clinton's critics, said, "You're just tiptoeing around the medical condition you're really upset about, one that she has that no other president in history has faced. Hillary Clinton has Chronic No-Penis. It's congenital . . . every woman in her family has had the same thing."

I've gotten pretty jaded about media sexism, but it's still amazing to me, however, that young female reporters like Kasie Hunt and Kristen Welker could participate regularly in discussions on people's perceptions of Clinton as "untrustworthy" without once questioning whether there just might be a few gendered projections, stereotypes, and expectations at work. It's so obvious to anyone who knows anything about mythology, fairy tales, or actual history—even fairly recent history, like that of the Clarence Thomas/Anita Hill hearings—that notions about the deceitfulness of women, as Sonya Chemaly put it, "resonate deeply in the cultural imagination," from Eve to the scheming housewives of "reality" television. But I will draw your attention to some very current evidence that there is a double standard when it comes to the perception of "trustworthiness":

In October 2015, a Suffolk University–*USA Today* poll asked people to list the terms they associate with the top presidential candidates. The words "liar," "dishonest," and "untrustworthy" were most associated with Clinton. Not surprising. More surprising, perhaps, is that those terms were also associated with Carly Fiorina, "a relative newcomer to politics and the only other woman in the race." In contrast, all of the male candidates, including Trump, were more likely to be called "honest" than "dishonest."

Two years ago, Anderson Cooper attempted to replicate a study out of NYU's Stern School of Business that had found that women in power are seen as "less trustworthy" than men in the same position. Cooper asked students to score one of two hypothetical executives who were described in exactly the same terms, except that one was called "Catherine" and the other "Mark." Catherine scored significantly lower than Mark when it came to "trust."

After Clinton gave her first press conference on the issue of her emails, *Business Outsider* assigned body language "expert" Christopher Hadnagy to decipher her non-verbal comportment. "I don't know if we have enough to say she is lying or telling the truth" (when asked about the emails), Hadnagy said, but he diagnosed "a high level of discomfort," noting such giveaways as lip licking and shoulder shrugging. When Clinton fidgeted with her notes, Hadnagy called the action that of a "manipulator." A few months later, another "expert," Dan Hill, commenting on another Clinton news conference, said she "seemed almost stunned at how long media focus has remained on the server issue." Her mouth often hung often, he pointed out, showing that "whatever she may have wanted to shield from public view by using her own email server, what Clinton can't hide is that she's now deeply discombobulated." Donald Trump's sniffing, grimacing, pouting? No one asked either expert to comment on the "meaning" of that. Or of Bernie Sanders's finger pointing and arm waving.

The interpretation of Clinton's body language was mild stuff, however, compared to the virulent misogyny of the T-shirts, memes, and shouts from the crowds at rallies:

"She lied. She's a liar!"

"Put her in prison!"

"She deserves to be in stripes!"

"Lock her up!"

No, it wasn't the audience at a trial for a child murderer. It was the Republican convention, and the crowd was hungry for blood. They cheered and clapped and shouted for vengeance as Pat Smith declared Hillary Clinton "personally responsible" for the death of her son during the raid at Benghazi, Libya. Outside the hall, T-shirts advising "Life's a Bitch; Don't Vote for One" were sold out; on Pinterest, over a thousand images and memes portrayed Clinton as a witch.

The witch/bitch memes weren't just from Trump supporters. They may have been the most unrestrained—incited by their candidate's own commitment to jail Hillary, should he win the election. But Bernie supporters held the "Hillary 2016 for Prison" signs up at their rallies, too, and "Bernie-Bros" tweeted at Hillary supporters that she was a "lying shit-bag" and in supporting her their "vaginas are making terrible choices." They harassed supporters at rallies, and unleashed special fury at female reporters. Sarah Jeong of *Vice* had to shut down her Twitter account after being flooded with sexist attacks, simply because she had asked Sanders supporters to tone down their rhetoric. Janell Ross of *The Washington Post* was inundated with "a variety of curse words and insults typically reserved for women. More than one has suggested that I deserve to become the victim of a sex crime."

Sanders himself, probably not wishing to alienate his fiercest supporters, was uncharacteristically mild in his response to the increasingly violent, misogynistic outbursts. "Senator Sanders is committed to running a positive campaign on the issues, and we encourage all of his supporters to stick to that same message," Hector Sigala, Sanders's digital media director, told *Mashable*. That's all you got, Bernie? Sanders had frequently declared himself an ardent feminist, but—unlike John McCain, who had sternly informed his own Islamophobic supporter of Obama's Christian religion and American citizenry—Bernie pretty much let his "Bros" do whatever they wanted. He claimed that he couldn't—and shouldn't—try to control what his supporters thought, but that, of course, was disingenuous nonsense. He knew he had tremendous influence, particularly with his younger fans, and exploited it throughout his campaign. But he never criticized the misogyny in their attacks on Clinton.

Trump: Mistaking Bluntness for Honesty

For several days at the beginning of July, I'd been watching the media pundits salivate over the previous week's poll results, in which Donald Trump rated sixteen points better than Hillary Clinton in a question asking which one was "better" at "being honest and straightforward." These astonishing results afforded the media an opportunity to chew yet again over "Hillary's honesty problem."

It never occurred to any of the pundits (or simply wasn't journalistically hot enough) to question the poll question itself, as in: Which quality did respondents have in mind? Truthfulness? Or straightforwardness? It is perfectly possible to lie in a straightforward way (the best liars, in fact, do so baldly), *or* to be truthful but not in a straightforward way—for example, when one is trying to tell someone something that will be hurtful or explain something complex or contradictory.

In fact, a good argument can be made that Trump is a perfect example of a straightforward liar, while Hillary has, after decades of concocted scandals, contributed to her "honesty problem" precisely because she has learned to speak the truth so cautiously that it seems phony. She also tries to be exact. Political commentators grow impatient with complex explanations about ever-changing classification procedures or differences between "marked" and "unmarked" emails; they glaze over when faced with the subtleties of her policies. They would rather take questions on the polls at face value than examine how they may lead or mislead.

It may also be, dictionary be damned, that saying whatever you feel like without regard for fact has come to be equivalent to "telling it like it is"—which in turn is conflated with honesty. So "straight shooter" Trump, who (unlike the circumspect, cautious Clinton) "told it like it is" (without regard for political correctness, people's feelings, or factual evidence) was for that reason seen as more honest. Hillary Clinton—who rarely lost her cool and only got truly aggressive with Trump after months of "lock her up!"—was seen, in contrast, as "inauthentic" and therefore "untrustworthy." We heard it virtually every day, not only from her political enemies, but from news commentators on every channel, who simply could not resist raising the issue, no matter how irrelevant it was to the main story they were reporting. We heard it in casual comments and jokes told by neighbors, as if it were an accepted scientific fact that needed no proof. We saw its influence on her approval numbers in the polls.

Commentators would now have us believe that the honesty issue didn't figure in much at all, that the desire for "change" and the strategic mistakes made by Clinton's team trumped everything else. But if that's the case, why did Hillary's accelerating momentum stall so dramatically eleven days before the election, when James Comey's revival of the email "scandal" upstaged the twelve women accusing Trump of sexual violations, and reminded voters, once again, of the specter of "lying Hillary"?

The Degeneration of the Mainstream Media

Throughout the 2016 primary and general elections, I was immensely grateful for those investigative reporters—Kurt Eichenwald, David Farenholdt, Ezra Klein, David Corn, among others—who worked so hard to separate fact from spin, to find the truth behind the phony "scandals," and to unearth the actual crimes and misdemeanors perpetrated by the campaigns. I never miss an interview with Joy Reid—or her weekend *AM Joy* show; I know I can count on her to hold the surrogates' and campaign managers' feet to the fire when they start to meander and trip around the truth. But for some time now, the mainstream media has been as much a facilitator of political fictions as the watchdog that keeps the spinmeisters honest.

Daniel Boorstin, way back in the sixties, predicted this turn. Mass media, he warned, generates "pseudo-events." A pseudo-event is something that acquires its authority not because it is accurate, but simply because the media has reported it, repeated it, exaggerated it, replayed it, made a mantra of it. A classic early example is security guard Richard Jewell, who was wrongly accused of being the pipe bomber at the Atlanta

Olympics in 1996. Exploiting the possibilities of a great story—"The Hero Turned Suspect"—reporters zestfully painted
a portrait of him to fit the "profile" of a "lone bomber," a frustrated police "wannabe" who—the coup de grâce—had duct
tape under his bed and curtains drawn in his house. No real
evidence against him existed, but the constructed journalistic "text" was so coherent and convincing—and the duct tape,
in particular, made into such a compelling detail—that it was
all people talked about for weeks. He was ultimately exonerated, but the exoneration didn't make the headlines (the truth
can be so boring!) and many people today still think he was
the bomber.

The same thing has happened, time and again, with Clintonian "scandals," from Whitewater to Benghazi to the "private server" to the Clinton Foundation. The GOP would seize
on anything that didn't "look quite right" or could be made to
appear that way, begin a major investigation, and announce
their suspicions to the press in a way that emphasized (or
concocted) potentially "criminal" or "unethical" behavior.
The press, doing what they believe is their job and getting a
good story in the process, take it all straight to the headlines
as "breaking news," at which point it's on every ticker and
is hotly discussed on every major show. When no damning
facts are found to confirm the stories, they may (or may not)
be retracted . . . but by then, the story is already circulating "in
the air." Like members of a jury who are instructed to strike
something that's been objected to in court, there's no really
effective "walking back" of what we've heard.

It's really hard to dislodge or discredit a pseudo-event
once people have heard it enough times. As Laurel Raymond
and Josh Israel wrote in August: "As a theory spreads—even if
it gets debunked at various points along the way—sheer den-

sity confers a sense of 'truthiness,' to borrow an apropos term from Stephen Colbert." I would add, too, that people have an investment in being "in the know" when it comes to common wisdom. It makes them feel "informed," part of an engaged community that's on top of things. This was true of Sanders supporters, who would recite the same list of Sanders talking points over and over. And it was true of Trump enthusiasts, who were proud to be among those who saw through Hillary's crimes, who weren't afraid to call her out, political correctness be damned.

Throughout the 2016 election, the pseudo-event ruled the airwaves, especially on the rolling news channels where leaks, poll results, gaffes, "optics," and concocted "scandals" were immediately turned into high-voltage headlines and endlessly repeated, organizing people's perceptions into yet-to-be-analyzed "narratives" of dubious factual status. In the process, like a piece of trashy gossip that has made the rounds of the high school cafeteria, "untrustworthy Hillary" became stamped in viewers' or readers' minds as a naturally occurring fact, rather than a perception that had been pushed deliberately by her enemies and inadvertently by the media.

Sexism may have provided the fertile soil, and the GOP may have planted the seeds and cultivated them through their endless attacks, investigations, and hearings—but it took the media's continual harping on Hillary's "trust issues" to turn them into the (pseudo-) realities that they are today. It's been so easy: present every charge by the GOP as "breaking news," report every new email find as a potential treasure trove of hidden secrets, remind viewers that "people don't trust her" every chance you get, and by the time a pollster calls and asks, the "trust problem" shows up as a documented "fact."

Consider: Some ordinary Joe or Jane is eating her Jimmy Dean muffin sandwich and the telephone rings.

"How would you rate Hillary Clinton on trustworthiness?" a bland voice asks (after numbing the recipient with dozens of other questions). Joe or Jane probably hasn't independently researched the issues involved, but has heard the words repeated, over and over, on the morning and evening news: "Hillary's trust issue." And then, too, there are all those scandals, and investigations, and emails . . . and, hmmm . . . come to think of it, why would the question even be asked if there wasn't something to it?

"I guess I don't think she's very trustworthy, no."

No, I don't think it's a conspiracy. And I would never describe the media, as Donald Trump does, as an "opposition party" who are deliberately dishonest. I have a great deal of sympathy for the challenges they face. For a start, they are dealing with extremely slippery, often highly unethical partisan perspectives. "Breaking news" comes at them fast and furious. And—as I will discuss at more length shortly—they are trying to present reliable information in a culture that is increasingly uninterested in getting at the facts. I don't see the media as the enemy; I believe reporters are doing what they think is their "job."

But it's also true that the reporters' notion of what their "job" is has changed, gradually but inexorably, since the 1950s and 1960s when the anchors—like Edward R. Murrow and Walter Cronkite—were recruits from print journalism. Men like Cronkite, who believed in reportage that "required careful examination through text," were skeptical about the informational value of such a visually oriented format as television; if you compared a man who spent a year reading the newspaper with one who watched TV news, Cronkite once commented, "the guy who had been watching television would come out with a damn strange idea of what happened in the world."

But by the late sixties, producers like Don Hewitt, who introduced *60 Minutes*, were experimenting with "packaging reality as well as Hollywood packages fiction." People, Hewitt believed, "were interested in seeing Morley, Dan, and Mike pursue a story, just as they like to see Kojak." The line between informing and entertaining was becoming blurrier. At the same time, the advent of CNN and its other twenty-four-hour-news-cycle spawn created the need both to fill time and hold viewers captive, resulting in too-swift reporting and endless sensationalizing repetition of the latest "breaking news"—giving uncertain reports the illusion of "truthiness."

"The inevitable result," as television historian Steven Stark remarks in *Glued to the Set*, "was a thinner line between fact and rumor."

All these factors were in play during both the 2008 and 2012 elections. But with the 2016 election, it seems, several new developments made the line between fact and rumor, truth and "story," even thinner—and profoundly strengthened the resilience of the "Untrustworthy Hillary" fiction.

Optics

First, "Bad Optics" became a prominent topic of political punditry, and eventually began to be discussed as though it were a crime in itself. Case in point: the August 30 *New York Times* editorial recommending that the Clinton Foundation be shut down immediately. It's a prime example of how the pseudo-issue of Clinton's "trust problem" was perpetuated through the authority of appearances rather than facts. And it happens entirely in the first two paragraphs:

> Does the new batch of previously undisclosed State Department emails prove that big-money donors to the Bill, Hillary & Chelsea Clinton Foundation got special favors from Mrs. Clinton while she was secretary of state?
>
> **Not so far, but that the question arises yet again** points to a need for major changes at the foundation now, before the November election.

Let me point out a few things. First, the use of the term "batch." The number of "undisclosed" emails ("related to" Benghazi—in what way, who knows?) was actually thirty out of thirty-three thousand—not exactly an overflowing cornucopia of evidence.

More significant, the answer to the question as to whether this "batch" "proves" that "big-money donors . . . got special favors from Mrs. Clinton" is, note carefully, *"Not so far."* A simple "no" would have proved sufficient, and would be completely factual. But the *Times* couldn't resist adding that loaded, suggestive "so far," implying that perhaps—indeed, perhaps likely—something suspect will show up later. There was no reason to suspect this, as nothing of significance had shown up. It's pure insinuation. Stay tuned!

Having established (again, through insinuation) that "special favors" may yet be discovered, the *Times* can then go on to speak as though their own speculation has the weight of proven fact. "That the question arises yet again points to a need . . ." The grammar makes it sound as though the question of special favors arose by itself, crystallizing out of thin air, when in fact it's the *Times* itself that is raising the question. It's the *Times*, not the "question," that is doing the "pointing" here.

Is the appearance of a conflict of interest important to investigate? Of course. But until the "appearance" is discovered to rest on fact, it's premature to call for "major changes"—as the wording of this article recommends with urgency.

In fact, multiple investigations into the whole "Clinton Foundation Scandal" never produced any evidence of "pay for play." But, as I'll discuss in more detail later, it remained a story, as reporters described the "mere possibility of 'impropriety' as a form of corruption."

False Equivalences Became the New Standard of "Objectivity"

"Clinton says Trump Leading Hate Movement; he calls her a 'bigot'"; that was the storyline for a piece in CNN *Politics*, in which Theodore Schleifer and Jeremy Diamond likened Hillary Clinton's "Alt-Right" speech, which provided a wealth of detail linking Trump's campaign to white supremacist groups, to Donald Trump calling Hillary a "bigot" for pursuing the African American vote. The equivalence? Each is calling the other a racist.

"Trump, Clinton both threaten free press." That's a headline from *USA Today*. How do they "both threaten the free press"? Trump has banned news organizations hostile to him and basically considers reporters a bunch of liars. Hillary?

She's uncomfortable with press conferences. (Erik Wemple of *The Washington Post* writes with irony that a more accurate version of the "equivalence" would have been: "Trump poses mortal threat to First Amendment, Clinton prone to secrecy.")

Chuck Todd of *Meet the Press* predicted on May 3, 2016 that the following six months would see "the two most unpopular people running for president, probably going down a low road, led by Trump—Clinton feeling, doing the same thing, and it's sort of this race to the bottom." The notion that there was any indication Clinton would—or could, by dint of her more reserved personality—take a road as low as Trump's is absurd. But for many journalists, such "balancing" of the scales—what Paul Krugman has called "bothsidesism"—is now seen as "objective" reporting.

"Yes, Trump is a raving lunatic, but what about those emails?" That one I made up. But it pretty much sums up the kind of "balance" that prevailed during the 2016 election, captured most succinctly, according to Erik Wemple, by Matthew Dowd's November 1 tweet: "Either you care both about Trump being sexual predator & Clinton emails, or u care about neither. But don't talk about one without the other."

Suspicion as the "Go-To" Approach to Telling Stories

This is one that seems to have been applied to Clinton far more often than to any other candidate, as we saw in the way Clinton's pneumonia was handled by the press, when her "penchant for privacy" (as *The New York Times* put it) "threaten[ed] to make her look, again, as though she has something to hide," while Trump's ludicrous doctor's letter was laughed about—and then forgotten.

Clinton's "motives," too, were constantly questioned during the election:

"One thing we need to recognize about Clinton's speech on race is how it turned the conversation away from questions about the Clinton Foundation."

Yes, Kasie Hunt really tried to make this the main topic of a panel about Clinton's "Alt-Right" speech. It was a brilliant and well-aimed warning, but Hunt was determined to find something suspect about the very fact that it was so news-worthy. While Al Sharpton was able to return the discussion to the troubling racial dynamics of Trump's campaign, he wasn't there later in the day when other reporters took the same tack as Hunt. Apparently, the more compelling Clinton's speeches, the more likely they are to have been devised to "divert" us from the "scandals" that defined her campaign.

"Perception" Made into Reality

The polls did this all the time, by wording questions that were supposedly only about "perceptions" in such a way that they implied the accuracy of those perceptions. And in constantly reporting poll results without examining their biases, the media perpetuated the myth of the polls' objectivity. In a July NBC–*Wall Street Journal* survey, for example, the first item in a list of "four criticisms that have been made about Hillary Clinton"—which respondents were asked to rank as either "a serious concern or not"—reads: "She has a record of being dishonest and is not trustworthy." The wording of the prompt presents Clinton's dishonesty as an established fact. I wonder how many of the 69 percent who found the trust criticism a "serious concern" were at least a little influenced by being "reminded" of the "record" of dishonesty?

Narrative and Image Replace Fact

Whereas programs like *60 Minutes* traditionally made "stories" the coat hanger on which the news was presented to the viewer (and reporters got in trouble if their stories were proven false), by 2016 the stories themselves had become the invisible thread that bound the "news" together, and when they unraveled, reporters didn't even notice. So, during the election, polls were constantly trotted out showing Hillary as historically "unpopular," with "unfavorables" equal to Trump's. That was the dominant "narrative" and one that served the media very well, as it created the impression of a neck-and-neck horserace, and kept viewers tuned in for the latest results.

It doesn't square very well, however, with the huge popular vote advantage Clinton won in the election. Have we seen this disparity explored or analyzed? On the contrary, now that the media has decided that Clinton was a "flawed candidate," "an imperfect messenger" who lacked dynamism or a good campaign strategy, there's rarely any mention of the overwhelming popular vote advantage—nearly three million—that Hillary finished with. It doesn't fit the current narrative. Did the media pile-on concerning her emails, the "common wisdom" about her unpopularity, the "appearance of impropriety" in the Clinton Foundation have nothing to do with her loss? Entertaining that would require some media self-scrutiny, which is the one "narrative" that never seems to take hold.

I've become quite old-fashioned in my attitude toward facts. When I was in college in the sixties, I, like many of my generation, was frustrated by the arrogance of those who claimed to be in possession of "truth." Thomas Kuhn's *The Structure of Scientific Revolutions* (1962), which introduced the notion that science was guided by accepted paradigms rather than a glimpse of unfiltered "reality," had only just been published. Academic feminism, which challenged the masculinist biases of dominant ideas about knowledge, didn't yet exist. The post-structuralist revolution, which had us deconstructing all claims to universal, objective, timeless truths, was barely beginning.

Over the next couple of decades, all that changed—mostly for the better, within the halls of academe. But outside those halls, knowledge was being deconstructed, too, and the results were not always so edifying. While academics studied Baudrillard and wrote papers about the world of "simulations," digital technology was taking over the world of image production and radically changing our notions of what a "real" human body looks like. The result: an epidemic of body-image disorders, as young women and men compared their real flesh to the perfected faux bodies on glossy magazine covers and learned how to alter their own photographs to present themselves in more flawless form on Instagram.

While academics challenged the notion that there is one version of history, Oliver Stone and others were producing accounts of the JFK assassination and Watergate scandal that are such an inseparable stew of fact and fantasy—all meshed together through the verisimilitude of film—that our students enter history class entirely befuddled about the most basic elements of "what happened." As the technology of image-making has become more and more sophisticated, the films look more and more like documentaries, and careful attention to the details of historical "accessories" has made revisionist cinematic history much more seductive and powerful.

Perhaps most dangerous in this "post-fact" society has been the dismissal of scientific evidence (for example, concerning climate change) as "opinion"—or even (as Trump declared) as "a hoax" created by the Chinese in order to make U.S. manu-facturing non-competitive. On the basis of a complete repudi-ation of the scientific evidence, Trump thus plans to "cancel" the Paris climate agreement—a move that 376 members of the National Academy of Sciences claim would produce "severe and long-lasting consequences for our planet's climate and the for the international credibility of the United States." His presidency, as the editors of *Scientific American* note, would take "antiscience to previously unexplored terrain."

As of this writing, we do seem to be finally becoming aware of the dangers of a "post-fact" culture. Most of the alarm, however, is centered on Trump's bald-faced lies and his min-ions' attempts to justify them as "alternative facts" or "not to be taken literally." Trump is indeed outrageously scornful of evidence or argument. But we would make a big mistake to not recognize that disdain for fact has been creeping up on us for some time, preparing our receptivity to the Big Con that so many Americans just fell for.

I remember during the O. J. Simpson trial, for example, being astounded when one juror dismissed the DNA evidence as "just a waste of time. It was way out there and carried no weight with me." Impressionist snapshots, in contrast, *did* carry weight. Detective Philip Vannnatter, as one juror explained, didn't look jurors in the eyes and thus couldn't be trusted. The accuracy of criminologist Henry Lee's findings, however, were certified for another juror by the warm smile he directed at the jury as he approached the witness stand to testify. Simpson himself was declared innocent by one of my students at the time because "he's a football hero, and handsome, and seems nice and friendly, and, well, I just sort of see it that way."

This kind of thinking created enormous benefits for Trump, who himself is "post-truth" and was able to snooker journalists into going along with him. It's true that he was indulged, in part, because he wasn't initially taken seriously as a candidate; his status as a celebrity (not a politician, whose motives would be more suspect) also won him a very different kind of treatment, allowing him countless phone-in interviews on shows like *Morning Joe*, where he schmoozed amiably and was never taken to task for his lies and extremism. I also believe, however, that people who were familiar with his pre-election personae never quite believed he was as vile as he seemed in his campaign speeches. That is, the character that Donald Trump created for himself on *Celebrity Apprentice* remained an invisible but highly influential presence during the campaign, even as candidate Trump was shouting messages of hate, bigotry, and misogyny from the stump. Contrary to the beliefs of those who never watched the show—which was undoubtedly most of the pundits— Trump did not often bark "You're fired!" in a cold and heartless way. Rather, he usually preceded his celebrity firings with praise and issued his conclusion reluctantly. His role, throughout, was that of a wise, fatherly, somewhat stern yet dependably rational boss. While the contestants competed ruthlessly and often nastily with each other—always with at least one loose canon in the bunch—Trump and his children appeared, in contrast, as calm, businesslike managers. When Trump began to talk about building walls and deporting immigrants, those who Clinton referred to as "the deplorables" among his supporters may have been rooting for these policies. But an equal number, I believe, never really believed in bigoted, racist Trump, who was so strikingly different from the dignified manager they had come to know through *Celebrity Apprentice*.

That was one persona. Then, for months during the primary, all we heard was what a "straight shooter" Trump was, how "authentic," how he "told it like it is." This became the favored Trump "narrative" for so long that no one bothered to worry whether anything he said was true or not. Some have suggested that it's because there are just too many lies to keep track of; the poor commentators, flooded with material, don't know where to start. There's something to this, but there is also—and more deeply important, I think—the perfect concordance between Trump and our postmodern world, in which the relevant question is rarely "Is it true or false?" but rather "How is it playing?" So, when then-candidate Trump returned from a frantic, unplanned trip to Mexico, cable commentators spoke of whether the "stagecraft" was successful and asked if Trump's standing side by side with the Mexican president Peña Nieto "moved the needle" of people's perceptions. Of far less interest to them was whether Trump had spoken the truth, either about what went on during his discussion with Peña Nieto (which it seems he did not: Trump said they had not discussed payment of his "signature" wall, while Nieto said he had "made it clear" that Mexico would not pay) or in his greatly exaggerated claims about immigrant crime later at his Arizona rally.

In this world of optics and appearances, pundits stopped wondering about who the "real" Trump was, and became more interested in charting or predicting "reboots," "resets," and "pivots." "Can they pitch this new look?" Katty Kay, a British correspondent who has become a *Morning Joe* regular, summed this up as the "challenge" facing a "softer" side of Trump that seemed at one point to be emerging, thanks to the restylings of the crafty Republican-operative-turned-campaign-manager Kellyanne Conway. "This is the kind of Trump," said Michael Steele at the time, who can challenge the Democrats and, indeed, might win the election. Only Donnie Deutsch, the ad man (who perhaps knows a bit himself about pitching and selling), raised the issue of whether or not the latest Trump "do-over" was to be trusted. We have some good evidence, by now, that it wasn't; what was touted as a "pivot" turned out to be a blip.

When did media journalism go so postmodern on us? Actually, it's been moving in that direction for a long time; as political campaigns have become more and more like theater, reporters have begun to adopt the role of theater critics rather than investigative journalists. Unfortunately, most of them aren't very good at discerning what literature professors call "unreliable narrators." Nor are they very adept at analyzing and deconstructing the dramatic texts presented to them. They've adopted the sexy language of "optics," "narrative," and so on—but without the critical tools to separate the fictional from the factual. For many journalists, doing that simply isn't seen as part of the job description any longer. Others, happily, are calling for the revival of old-style investigative journalism, and more and more are beginning to practice it. It's essential. For unless fictions and optical illusions like "Untrustworthy Hillary" and "Straight-shooter Trump" are deconstructed, they will continue to be recycled and reinforced—and their status, over time, transformed from pseudo-realities into fact.

Wait, forget "over time"; they have already been engraved as fact in the minds of millions of Americans.

5.

Damned Emails

Here's a shocker: Clinton didn't lie about "the damned emails." Nor did she treat classified material in an "extremely careless" manner. The email "scandal," like many previous investigations into the Clintons, was a whole lot of nothing blown to nuclear proportions by the GOP and helpfully served up in an endless stream of tasty, poisonous portions by the mainstream media. For weeks, we snacked on high-calorie accusations and insinuations—including some delivered personally by Vladimir Putin via WikiLeaks. And then, just as we appeared to be stuffed to the brim and our attention had turned to the Trumpish behavior that had shaken Michelle Obama (and thousands of other American women) to her core, we were presented with a flaming dessert, courtesy of James Comey.

Part One: A Scandal is Born

On October 22, 2015 Hillary Clinton made her final, triumphant appearance before the neverending Benghazi Committee. The hearings had been plodding on since September

2014, trying to pin responsibility on Clinton for the death of Christopher Stevens and three other Americans. But her day-long October interrogation should have ended it; it was an extraordinary event and a dazzling performance, in which Clinton, as Politico's Edward Isaac Dovere describes her, "delivered tirelessly, knocking back the Republicans one by one" and "reminded people of everything they like about her: toughness, but also a calm, adult presence of someone you can actually see being president of the United States."

Chairman Trey Gowdy, who had "been conducting the investigation like an overzealous prosecutor desperately trying to land a front-page conviction rather than a neutral judge of facts seeking to improve the security of our diplomatic core" was not to be defeated, however. For just as one investigation into Bill Clinton had led to another . . . and another . . . and another, the Benghazi investigators, asking for some emails, had struck an unexpected new fountain of perpetually flowing liquid gold for their purposes.

On March 2, 2015 *The New York Times*'s Michael Schmidt made it public for the first time: the Benghazi hearings had revealed that Clinton "exclusively used a personal email account to conduct government business as secretary of state." "Hillary Clinton Used Personal Email Account at State Dept., Possibly Breaking Rules" read the headline. In the piece itself, Schmidt described Clinton's "expansive use" of the private account as "alarming" and "a serious breach," and noted that Clinton and her aides had also failed to retain her letters and emails as required by federal law.

"Breaking Rules" was, of course, a dog whistle for Clinton scandal seekers. We had been told so many times that she and Bill live by "rules of their own" that the piece hardly required fact-checking. Or did it?

The truth is that there was no "serious breach." In 2009, when Clinton was secretary of state, Federal Register regulations pertaining to the use of emails specifically allowed "employees of certain agencies," including the State Department, "to use non-Federal email systems." That's why Secretary of State Colin Powell did so, and did not advise Clinton against doing so. It was only in 2013, *after Clinton had left office,* that the "rules" were changed. The National Archives updated their guidelines to say that employees should generally use personal email accounts only in "emergency situations," in which cases all of the emails must be preserved "in accordance with agency recordkeeping practices." According to those practices, however, it was not the responsibility of the secretary of state or her aides to preserve her emails, but the State Department itself—which it did. (That's how those not submitted by her were later "discovered".)

In 2013—again, to be clear, after Clinton had left office—the State Department asked all former secretaries of state to provide copies of work-related emails from personal accounts. No one except Clinton did. Clinton: "I responded right away and provided all my emails that could possibly be work related, which totaled roughly fifty-five thousand printed pages, even though I knew that the State Department already had the vast majority of them."

It was totally legitimate, by the way, for Clinton and her lawyers to delete her personal emails from the stack submitted to the State Department, as the Justice Department made crystal clear in May 2016, when the conservative watchdog group Judicial Watch brought a lawsuit. "There is no question," the Justice Department's civil division attorneys wrote, "that former Secretary Clinton had authority to delete personal emails without agency supervision—she appropriately could have done so even if she were working on a government server."

But this was Hillary Clinton, after all, queen of political duplicity. Who knows what those deleted private emails were "shielding"? On March 3, Schmidt followed up his March 2 story, describing Clinton as engaging in a practice that "protected a significant amount of her correspondence from the eyes of investigators and the public." He quoted Jeff Bechdel, spokesperson for America Rising, a conservative PAC that produces opposition research on Democratic Party members:

> Unfortunately, Clinton's own political calculation and desire for secrecy, as evidenced by her exclusive use of personal email accounts while at State, is preventing an open process and full, fair review of her time there.

Bechdel was a GOP spokesperson. There was no "evidence" tying Clinton's use of a personal email to "political calculation" or a "desire for secrecy." This was clearly a narrative that reporter Schmidt felt no obligation to correct. Indeed, in his own editorializing the day before, he had said much the same thing, only using more cautious journalistic euphemisms, like "echoes" instead of "as evidenced":

> The revelation about the private email account echoes longstanding criticisms directed at both the former sec-

retary and her husband, former President Bill Clinton, for a lack of transparency and inclination toward secrecy.

"Echoes" is not synonymous with "as evidenced by"—if you are taking the SATs. But for the casual reader, skimming the story on a commuter train or while eating breakfast, what undoubtedly stood out were the phrases "lack of transparency" and "inclination toward secrecy." They were such familiar ingredients in the coverage of "The Clintons"—and quickly became headlined in every story. Within a week, Clinton's emails had become an emerging "scandal" that sidelined all her attempts to talk about policy. The coverage was full of rhetorical flourishes that threw shade on the Clintons' "past"—the details of which few readers/viewers, particularly if they were young, were actually familiar with: "Can she reinvent herself or will she be forever dogged by how she has approached controversies in the past?" "Even friendly Democrats wondered whether she and her team were capable of turning over a new leaf." Clinton, struggling to figure out how to explain the complexities of what we now know was an archaic, clumsy, contradictory system of record keeping, was chastised for being slow to answer the charges. She had "allowed the controversy to swelter for days." Would she now finally "show contrition?"

Contrition was not something that Clinton owed anyone, as she hadn't done anything wrong. But Representative Trey Gowdy, the South Carolina Republican who was chairing the House panel investigating the attack on the U.S. embassy in Benghazi, felt otherwise. Salivating over this fresh opportunity to bring Clinton down, he said he planned to haul the former secretary of state in for hearings "at least twice."

Gowdy also said he saw "no choice" but for Clinton to hand her server to an independent arbiter who would sort through her emails and decide which of them should be made public. "Secretary Clinton alone created this predicament, but she alone does not get to determine its outcome," he said.

Later the same day, CNN's John King ran a piece called "Hillary Clinton's email scandal is exactly what you can expect from her presidential campaign":

> Secrecy. Shielding documents. Accusations of arrogance and hypocrisy. Debates about the letter and the spirit of the rules. A public defense—but also jitters and disbelief—from fellow Democrats. Legitimate criticism along with some eye-rolling conspiracy theories from Republicans. We have seen this movie before . . .
>
> What is past is prologue.

Yes, if you are determined to tell the story that way.

Part Two: Clinton Becomes a "Criminal" (Courtesy of *The New York Times*)

On July 23, 2015, the year before the election, the *Times* ran a story entitled "Criminal Inquiry Sought in Hillary Clinton's Use of Email." It began with the lede: "Two inspector generals have asked the Justice Department to open a criminal investigation into whether Hillary Clinton mishandled sensitive government information on a private email account she used as Secretary of State, senior government officials said Thursday."

The Facts: As Representative Elijah E. Cummings—Ranking Member of the House Committee on Oversight and Government Reform—and the Justice Department immediately confirmed, there was no "criminal inquiry" at all, but rather a review under the Freedom of Information Act of whether some emails not previously marked "classified" ought to have been. This had nothing to do with Clinton herself, and certainly didn't constitute a "criminal referral."

The *Times* later changed the headline and the lede, but insisted the story didn't require an explicit correction, allowing those who had seen the original headline—including early morning news–show pundits—a full day to run with the misguided impression that Clinton was under criminal investigation. Ultimately, the *Times* printed a correction, admitting that their story had "misstated the nature of the referral to the Justice Department regarding Hillary Clinton's personal email account when she was Secretary of State. The referral addressed the potential compromise of classified information in connection with that personal email account. It did not specifically request an investigation into Mrs. Clinton."

Barely anyone noticed the correction. It's the way these things tend to work. Headlines make the front page; retractions are buried. The consequences of this asymmetry can be devastating.

Part 3: Clinton Is Vindicated, but No One Knows It

Skip ahead to the presidential campaign. While Trump was given a free ride by the mainstream media and Sanders's "momentum" was the big narrative about his campaign, the "email scandal" became the dominant Clinton story of the year that followed.

Although no evidence existed that she was hiding anything, Hillary continued to be criticized for "not coming clean." She maintained, as she had at the February 2016 presidential debate, that she "never sent or received any classified material" and, in a press conference in May, that regarding the private server, "What I had done was allowed, it was above board." But reporters badgered her for more. They wanted contrition, an apology for her use of a private server—and ultimately, Clinton gave it, in a September 8 interview with David Muir on ABC:

> In retrospect, certainly, as I look back on it now, even though it was allowed, I should've used two accounts. One for personal, one for work-related emails. That was a mistake. I'm sorry about that. I take responsibility.

The next day she repeated that she did not "send or receive classified material on the private account." *USA Today* described the apology as an "about-face."

On May 26, however, Clinton was vindicated when the State Department inspector general released its eighty-three page evaluation of email management. Its major criticism, as Rachel Maddow reported—and visually demonstrated with a huge, unwieldy stack of paper—was reserved for the "archaic archiving system" that Clinton had to work with: an "abysmal system of record-keeping" in which the only approved method for archiving emails was by printing and boxing each one that was received or sent. No indexing or electronic storage, just physical "filing" of thousands and thousands of pages in box after box of printed emails.

Representative Cummings issued the following statement in response to the report:

> The Inspector General confirmed what we have known all along—that Secretary Clinton followed the practice of her predecessor when she used a personal email account. While Secretary Clinton preserved and returned tens of thousands of pages of her emails to the Department for public release, Secretary Powell returned none. Republicans need to stop wasting taxpayer dollars singling out Secretary Clinton just because she is running for President. If Republicans really care about transparency, they will work constructively with Democrats to focus on fixing what this report shows are longstanding, systemic flaws in the State Department's recordkeeping practices for decades.

Cummings's press release was substantiated by a piece in *Forbes* magazine, which concluded, that as regards Clinton's handling of emails, the evaluation "does not add any new serious charges or adverse facts" about Clinton but rather retraces a "dreary history of records and archival policy" involving "general problems" with printing and filing emails in a retrievable way that should not be "pinned" on Clinton. The piece concludes: "A report that says so little new against Clinton, amounts to a vindication."

But if Clinton was "vindicated" by the report, you certainly couldn't tell from the headlines and television tickers:

"Clinton's Violation of State Department Email Rules" (ticker on MSNBC)

"State Department Report Slams Clinton's Email Use" (CNN)

"State Dept. inspector general report sharply criticizes Clinton's email practices" (*Washington Post*)

"Hillary Clinton Is Criticized for Private Emails in State Dept. Review" (*New York Times*)

Part 4: James Comey's Abuse of Power, act I

On July 5, 2016, James Comey, director of the FBI, appeared on television to make an important, albeit befuddling, announcement: "Although we did not find clear evidence that Secretary Clinton or her colleagues intended to violate laws governing the handling of the classified information, there is evidence that they were extremely careless in their handling of very sensitive, highly classified information." Though he had cleared Clinton of all criminal charges, he had also ventured way beyond protocol in publicly criticizing Clinton and the State Department for their handling of classified emails, and recklessly speculating that her email system "could have been" hacked. The FBI's proper role is to conduct investigations into charges, which are then either dismissed or presented to and adjudicated by a judge or jury, *not* to publicly editorialize about conclusions. Comey's announcement was thus a stunning violation of Justice Department practice, which is to notify the public when an investigation is concluded, inform us of whether or not charges are brought, and then quietly leave the stage.

Not only did Comey abuse his power by chastising the behavior of a defendant who had been cleared of criminal charges, but he also left the listening public with the impression of a mixed verdict (which it was not; Clinton was cleared), and gave the GOP a heap of red meat to throw to the hungry media.

Besides the charge of "extreme carelessness," Comey also suggested that Clinton had lied, that—contrary to her statements to the public—she had received 110 classified emails (out of 30,000 the FBI had recovered). Clinton, of course, had claimed on television that she had neither received nor sent any classified emails on her private server. But she also clarified that she had meant "emails marked as classified." The clarification is crucial, because it's through a system of markings that the state department operates. The appropriate "header," as Ellen Tauscher, who served as an undersecretary in the State Department until 2012, corroborated, is *required* of all classified documents.

Of course, it's always possible for one person (or agency) to deem something "classified" and another person (or agency) to disagree. Indeed, that often happens, as documents travel from agency to agency and their contents get reinterpreted. Classification is a moving machine, which stopped at Clinton's desk marked in a particular way. She relied on those markings; how else could she—or anyone else in her position—operate?

FBI director James Comey, however, mentioned neither this nor the "archaic system" when he claimed that Clinton, contrary to her statements to the public, had received 110 classified emails. Classified? None of these emails had the required headers—so how was Clinton to know? Comey dismissed that as a triviality, claiming that the emails contained "subject matter" that "any reasonable person should have known . . . had no place in an unclassified system."

The media gave about five minutes to the fact that Clinton was cleared of any criminal activity in her handling of emails. The far hotter story was her "carelessness"—and, of course, the implication (not stated by Comey) that she had "lied to the public." Without allowing themselves a moment to examine Comey's words with care or to question his reckless breach of protocol, commentators immediately began to weave his report into their favored narrative of Clintonian "untrustworthiness."

"It's a complete political indictment of her conduct," declared MSNBC journalist Kristen Welker. "A direct disputation of the stories she's been telling," added political commentator Chris Cillizza. It demonstrated that "trust and honesty continue to dog the Clinton campaign" (Chuck Todd). Claiming that Coney had "completely disputed Hillary's claims," Andrea Mitchell predicted "grave political problems" for Clinton.

By the time Joe Scarborough, Mika Brzezinski, and Nicole Wallace got in on the act on *Morning Joe*, it had predictably become a tale of bald-faced deception on Clinton's part. The show began with artfully arranged side-by-side clips contrasting Clinton's statements with Comey's "assessments." Guests who tried to caution against hurried conclusions, like Steve Rattner and Howard Dean, were interrupted and talked over. Nothing was allowed to interfere with the "untrustworthy Clinton" thread.

Part 5: Comey is Forced to Retract His Criticism, but the Press Doesn't Notice

On July 7, 2016 House Republicans, unhappy with Comey's failure to indict Clinton, had asked him to answer questions from them, to which he agreed. Grilling him, they got little more than a slight elaboration of the initial "extremely careless" assessment:

Certainly she should have known not to send classified information. As I said, that's the definition of negligent. I think she was extremely careless. I think she was negligent. That I could establish. What we can't establish is that she acted with the necessary criminal intent.

But when Democrats took over the questioning, things got rockier for Comey. First, Elijah Cummings pressed Comey to restate, more explicitly, that only 3 of those 110 emails had any kind of markings on them at all which would have alerted the recipient to their classified status. Those three, moreover, were marked (mistakenly, as it later turned out) only "internally," with tiny letter symbols pertaining to specific sentences within the emails.

Then, Congressman Matt Cartwright forced Comey to admit that the emails with the internal *c*'s were not properly marked according to the State Department Manual, and that his previous comment that "any reasonable person" would have known the emails were classified was implausible, if not a out-and-out falsehood. To judge unheaded emails as classified was in fact a standard that was unreasonable to apply. To the contrary, it would be a "reasonable inference" that the three documents missing the header were *not* classified.

Holding the manual in his hand, Cartwright calmly got right to the point:

MATT CARTWRIGHT: You were asked about markings on a few documents, I have the manual here, marking national classified security information. And I don't think you were given a full chance to talk about those three documents with the little c's on them. Were they properly documented? Were they properly marked according to the manual?

JAMES COMEY: No.

MATT CARTWRIGHT: According to the manual, and I ask unanimous consent to enter this into the record, Mr. Chairman.

CHAIRMAN: Without objection so ordered.

CARTWRIGHT: According to the manual, if you're going to classify something, there has to be a header on the document? Right?

COMEY: Correct.

CARTWRIGHT: Was there a header on the three documents that we've discussed today that had the little c in the text someplace?

COMEY: No. There were three e-mails, the c was in the body, in the text, but there was no header on the email or in the text.

CARTWRIGHT: So if Secretary Clinton really were an expert about what's classified and what's not classified and we're following the manual, the absence of a header would tell her immediately that those three documents were not classified. Am I correct in that?

COMEY: That would be a reasonable inference.

Comey's admission exonerated Hillary not only from any "carelessness" or "negligence," but also from the charge of lying about "not sending or receiving any classified emails." It would have been entirely "reasonable" for her to conclude that the emails not appropriately marked were *not* classified— exactly as she had been saying for months.

If you were watching the hearing it was a revelatory moment. But how many viewers caught the exchange? Audiences at my talks, when I ran video clips of Cummings's and Cartwright's questioning, were shocked and amazed.

As for me, the hearing solidified my suspicion that Comey's unprecedented interference was indeed politically motivated (or pressured). For, surely at this point, Comey ought to have held a full-blown press conference apologizing for his inaccurate assessment of Clinton's handling of classified material. Instead, he was silent, while the media incessantly hammered away at Clinton's "carelessness" and "lies" about her emails. It was a recklessly disseminated narrative with no basis in fact. Yet at the time his mischaracterization was disclosed, Comey offered no public correction or retraction of his previous commentary, which was left to do its political dirty work, unchallenged by the facts. Thus for any viewers relying on TV "news"—MSNBC as well as Fox—these exonerating exchanges never happened, because their importance was never turned into "breaking news" or a "headline" story.

In fact, the media dug its heels in even further on the "lying Clinton" issue. On August 1, the *Washington Post* gave Clinton four "Pinocchios" for trying to correct Chris Wallace in a *Fox News Sunday* interview on July 31. Wallace had said, inaccurately, that "FBI director James Comey, in the congressional hearing, said none of those things that you told the American public were true." Wallace was either uninformed or lying, for Comey had said nothing of the sort. Rather, he said that he wasn't "qualified to answer" the question of "whether Clinton had lied to the public." What he *did* feel qualified to answer was whether her answers to the FBI were truthful, and on that issue he had replied that "we have no basis to conclude that she lied."

What did Clinton reply that got her pantsuit set on fire? Instead of quoting Comey's lawyerly "no basis to conclude that she lied," she answered in terms ordinary people use. She said Comey had said, "her answers were truthful." She then went on to connect the dots between her FBI testimony and what she had said to the public, describing them as "consistent" with each other. Complicated, perhaps. Requiring a bit of thought on the part of listeners, yes. But a lie? Give us a break.

Yet the saga of "Lying Hillary and her emails" went on and on, perpetuated not only in the headlines but by the polls.

For example, take the July *Washington Post*–ABC News poll results showing that 56 percent of respondents felt the FBI was wrong in not charging Clinton, a result that had the GOP falling over itself with glee. Comey's irresponsible comments on Clinton's "carelessness," as Andrea Mitchell predicted, did cause big trouble for Clinton. But the poll didn't simply "measure" this, it perpetuated it. Here's how the survey phrased the question, repeating in it the same inappropriate and leading (and as it turns out, inaccurate) "editorializing" that Comey indulged in:

> As you may have heard, FBI Director James Comey has recommended not charging Hillary Clinton with a crime for her use of personal email while Secretary of State, saying she did not have any criminal intent. He also said Clinton was "extremely careless" in her handling of classified information in her personal email. Do you approve or disapprove of Comey's recommendation that Clinton should not be charged with a crime?

Consider, too, that even after Comey's exoneration, polling showed that 56 percent of Americans believed Clinton had indeed broken the law by relying on a personal email address, "with another 36 percent piling on to say the episode showed 'bad judgment' albeit not criminality." Those numbers are ghastly, considering—as demonstrated in this chapter—that she had in fact broken no laws or behaved carelessly; but they are unsurprising, given the overwhelming negative attention that network and cable news has paid to Clinton's emails—more airtime, as Matthew Yglesias reports, than to all policy issues combined. During the entire general election campaign, from June 7 to November 8, Clinton only led over Trump in quantity of media coverage four times: once was when she had pneumonia, once was during the DNC, and the other two were during and right after James Comey's announcements.

Thus, "a story that was at best of modest significance came to dominate the U.S. presidential election," creating a misleading impression of Clinton's character and competence and vastly overshadowing coverage of both her accomplishments and her policy proposals. Is it any wonder that so many people had a totally false impression of what a Clinton presidency would be like? Between Sanders labeling Clinton as a Wall Street lacky and the GOP obsession with her emails—both of which were lavishly covered by the mass media—the Clinton campaign was defined by negative sound bites. It wasn't the case that she had "no message"; she wasn't given the space to deliver it, as the email "scandal" swamped the media.

6.

A Tale of Two Conventions— and One Hot Mic

When Hillary became the first woman to win a major party's presidential nomination, the mass media had a brief love affair with the "history-making" moment. There wasn't much time to relax, however, in the soothing process of VP picking that followed. Trump was now raging about "Crooked Hillary Clinton," whom he described as a "world-class liar," "the most corrupt person ever to seek the presidency," and who "ran the State Department as her own personal hedge fund." Ignoring the facts disclosed at the eleven-hour Benghazi hearing, he described Chris Stevens as having been "left helpless to die as Hillary Clinton soundly slept in her bed." He frequently cited *Clinton Cash: The Untold Story of How and Why Foreign Governments and Businesses Helped Make Bill and Hillary Clinton Rich* to make the case that the Clintons had gotten rich from "disastrous trade deals" in exchange for huge donations.

Clinton Cash: The Untold Story of How and Why Foreign Governments and Businesses Helped Make Bill and Hillary Rich is one of a still-growing number of poorly researched, openly vicious books churned out by the right-wing fantasy factory of Clinton crime exposés, carrying titles like *Un-*

likeable, Crisis of Character, Guilty as Sin, Hillary's America, and *The Clintons' War on Women.* Along with the widespread dissemination of fake news stories published in the *National Enquirer* (whose CEO is a good friend of Trump's) and other right-wing tabloids and broadsheets, they comprise a kind of alt-right alt-reality that has formed many people's notions of who Hillary Clinton is. It's impossible to quantify just how influential the books, themselves filled with citations (if at all) by articles from *Breitbart* and other right-wing websites, have been. But we know that a contingent of the FBI demanded inquiries into the Clinton Foundation on the basis of *Clinton Cash* (which has now been made into a graphic novel). D'Souza's *Hillary's America,* a wicked fairy tale about Hillary, enabler of Bill Clinton's sexual perversions, spent weeks at the top of *The New York Times* bestseller list, bested only by *Crisis of Character: White House Secret Service Officer Discloses His Firsthand Experience with Hillary, Bill and How They Operate.* Do you think a chunk of the sales are to readers like me, ready to debunk the lies that litter its pages? Not even close. *Hillary's America*—and the "documentary" based on it—has an average of five stars from readers/viewers on amazon.com.

The July GOP convention was an all-out festival of Hillary hating. Trump had received a nice little assist in his branding of "crooked Hillary" when, on June 27, Bill Clinton found himself on the same tarmac in Arizona as Attorney General Loretta Lynch. He pulled a Bill Clinton and impulsively visited her airplane to chat. The GOP immediately launched into tirades about how this was a deliberate attempt to influence Lynch about the investigations into Clinton's emails, while the media got equally excited about the "optics" of the visit. According to Lynch, she and Bill discussed grandchildren, golf, and other personal topics: "There was no discussion on any matter pending before the Department or any matter pending with any other body. There was no discussion of Benghazi, no discussion of State Department emails." The only issue of political significance they discussed was Brexit. Lynch, at the time, believed the conversation innocuous; but, given the scrutiny that followed, she came to see that in the highly partisan atmosphere of the investigation, any schmoozing with Bill Clinton was a huge mistake. So on July 1 she recused herself from the case—leaving Comey with the final word on email matters. That, as we have seen, proved to be a decision of no small consequence.

On the more positive side, however, there was the Democratic National Convention from July 25–28—as much a celebration of love as the RNC was a festival of hate. The first night was rocky, as anti-Hillary hecklers disrupted the speeches of Al Franken, Cory Booker, and Sarah Silverman (who told them they were "being ridiculous"). They yelled "We Trusted You!" at Elizabeth Warren, who had enraged them by endorsing Hillary. But once Michelle Obama took the stage, her distinctive brand of authority took over. Looking straight at the "Bernie or Busters," she described how when Hillary didn't win the nomination in 2008 "she didn't pack up and go home" but instead, "as a true public servant," understood "that this is so much bigger than her own desires and disappointments." She then went on to praise Clinton, unstintingly and with urgency. Trump was never mentioned by name, but he was a looming presence nonetheless.

Particularly striking to me about the Democratic convention was an unprecedented focus—from Michelle Obama's reflections on the "heart of our hearts," her daughters, to the mothers who had lost their children to police violence, to the

9/11 victims, and ultimately to Chelsea Clinton herself—on the power of caring, of mothering. The RNC had been full of bile and poison. But at the DNC, for the first time "untrustworthy Hillary" was challenged. You had to be listening, however. If you were listening, you heard countless stories from people who were tended to, touched, and comforted by Hillary, and whose lives she followed through the years, not just for a photo shoot. You learned that Barack Obama is a damn good hugger. You heard a daughter radiating personal gratitude for her mother's attentiveness as a parent—not just a smooth advertisement for her accomplishments (as Ivanka Trump's had been for Donald Trump). And you heard a candidate who admitted that the "service" part of public service has always been easier for her than the "public" part. Much of that service probably came as a great surprise to many; like most mothering, it was unshowy, behind the scenes, and often unacknowledged, while the fictional she-devil scored points for the GOP and ratings for the media.

Bill Clinton, too, gave a speech. It began with a rendition of his first meeting with Hillary:

> In the spring of 1971, I met a girl. The first time I saw her, we were, appropriately enough, in a class on political and civil rights. She had thick blond hair, big glasses. Wore no makeup. And she exuded this strength of self-possession I found magnetic.
>
> After the class, I followed her out, intending to introduce myself. I got close enough to touch her back, but I couldn't do it. Somehow, I knew this would not be just another tap on the shoulder, that I might be starting something I couldn't stop.

And it ended—brilliantly, despite Bill's shaking hands and seeming frailty—with the admonition that the Hillary of the hate books, the fake news, and the RNC chants of "Lock her up!" was a fiction. A cartoon. Having praised Hillary's accomplishments and talents, and calling her "the best damn changemaker" in public service, he asked:

> So, what is up with this? Well . . . a real changemaker represents a real threat. So your only option is to create a cartoon. A cartoon alternative. Then run against the cartoon. Cartoons are two-dimensional. They're easy to absorb. Life in the world is complicated and real change is hard. And a lot of people even think it is boring. Good for you, because earlier today you nominated the real one.

Rachel Maddow, while applauding the ending, found the opening "shocking and weird" and "not a feminist way to start" the convention. Apparently, she didn't like the use of the term "girl" and heard disquieting sexual overtones in the reference to "something I couldn't stop." I've always appreciated Maddow's analytic approach to the news and her emphasis on historical context. In this case, however, her reaction was a reminder to me of the generation gap in perspective that separated those whose ideas about Bill Clinton were shaped largely by sexual scandal from those who have other memories than the pain he caused both Hillary and Monica, the mess he made for the country, or the policies that turned out to have consequences both he and Hillary would regret.

Younger women may look at Bill and see only a wobbly voiced old guy who took advantage of a young intern but no longer has the hunky looks to even make it imaginable.

Those of us who are a little older, however, may see him differently. And while I have no particular need to defend Bill Clinton, I think it's important, in the light of the false equivalences Trump tried to draw between Bill's behavior and his own attitudes toward women, that some history be injected here.

Back when Bill Clinton was first running for the nomination, watching him on television, my friend—a distinguished historian—and I turned to each other and said: "He'll be our first female president!" What were we thinking, you ask? It had something to do with the fact that he was the first politician of my own age who didn't ostentatiously parade his masculinity. It had something to do with the way he talked about his wife Hillary, and the way he looked at her, beaming with admiration and something like awe—the way Nancy Reagan looked at Ronnie. It had something to do with his wholehearted, unembarrassed feminism. And yes, there was something about him that seemed vulnerable, craving of affection.

When my friend and I said that about Bill, we hadn't read Toni Morrison's piece in *The New Yorker*, in which she recalled African American men "murmuring," in the middle of the Whitewater investigation, that "white skin notwithstanding, this is our first Black president." Morrison listed the "tropes of blackness" Clinton displayed: "single-parent household, born poor, working-class, saxophone-playing, McDonald's-and-junk-food-loving." And then she got to the heart of her piece: "When the President's body, his privacy, his unpoliced sexuality became the focus of persecution, when he was metaphorically seized and body-searched," the message was one black men understood. "No matter how smart you are, how hard you work, how much coin you earn for us, we will put you in your place." Later, in explaining what she mean by the phrase "first black president," she made it explicit: "I was deploring the way in which President Clinton was being treated, vis-à-vis the sex scandal that was surrounding him. I said he was being treated like a black on the street, already guilty, already a perp."

Like Morrison, I was much more appalled at the prurient, prying, puritanical invasion of Bill Clinton's private sexual life, *and* of his body and Monica Lewinsky's, than I was over anything he did. Those of you who didn't live through it would have to read *The Starr Report* to see just how salacious that investigation was. (The word *sex* or some variation of it appears 581 times in the 445-page report, while *Whitewater*, the "scandal" which the Office of the Independent Counsel was supposed to be investigating, was mentioned just 4 times.) Did Bill Clinton take advantage of his power and position in conducting an intimate relationship with a White House intern? Yes. But it's very clear from *Monica's Story* that Monica herself considers the FBI, Kenneth Starr, and media harassers to have been the bigger bullies in her life. The FBI terrorized her with threats of imprisonment; Starr dragged the most intimate details of her relations with Clinton into full public view, and the media described her alternately as a slutty "sex siren," a "sad, pathetic loser," and a "portly pepperpot" whose zaftig body was a sign of her "moral laxity."

As to the right wing's portrayal of Hillary as persecuting Monica, the only documented fact is that Hillary, in a private communication with a close friend, referred to Monica as a "narcissistic loony-tune"—which even Monica felt was forgivable under the circumstances. ("My first thought," Lewinsky writes, "as I was getting up to speed: If that's the worst thing she said, I should be so lucky.") "Lewinsky became a house-hold name equated with blow jobs," as Janet Reitman wrote in *Rolling Stone,* not because of Hillary but because of the troll-ing anti-Clinton press: Maureen Dowd, who called Lewinsky "ditsy," lacking in brains, and "predatory," and others who spent most of their coverage of Clinton's presidency pursu-ing stories that would humiliate him. Monica agreed with Hillary, by the way, that the investigation was part of a "vast right-wing conspiracy" of "malicious" and "evil-minded" people.

Trump Gets Slimed—by Himself

After the conventions, there were the debates, expected to be the oddest piece of political theater we had seen yet during the election cycle. And they were. During the first debate, on September 26, Trump sniffled his way through largely incoherent answers and constant interruptions of Hillary's calm, knowledgeable performance. Then, at the very end, she caught Trump completely off-guard with an unexpected ref-erence. Lester Holt was just about to ask his final question, when Clinton interjected, "One thing, Lester . . ."

HOLT: Very quickly, because we're at the final question now.
CLINTON: You know, he tried to switch from looks to
    stamina. But this is a man who has called women pigs,
    slobs, and dogs, and someone who has said pregnancy is
    an inconvenience to employers, who has said . . .
TRUMP: I never said that.
CLINTON: . . . women don't deserve equal pay unless they do
    as good a job as men.

TRUMP: I didn't say that.

CLINTON: And one of the worst things he said was about a woman in a beauty contest. He loves beauty contests, supporting them and hanging around them. And he called this woman "Miss Piggy." Then he called her "Miss Housekeeping," because she was Latina. Donald, she has a name.

TRUMP: Where did you find this? Where did you find this?

CLINTON: Her name is Alicia Machado.

TRUMP: Where did you find this?

CLINTON: And she has become a U.S. citizen, and you can bet...

TRUMP: Oh, really?

CLINTON: ... she's going to vote this November.

Trump was clearly discombobulated, and responded with what we now can recognize as a threat of things to come: Hillary had not been "nice" to him, and so the gloves were going to come off:

TRUMP: But you want to know the truth? I was going to say something...

HOLT: Please, very quickly.

TRUMP: ... extremely rough to Hillary, to her family, and I said to myself, "I can't do it. I just can't do it. It's inappropriate. It's not nice." But she spent hundreds of millions of dollars on negative ads on me, many of which are absolutely untrue. They're untrue. And they're misrepresentations. And I will tell you this, Lester. It's not nice. And I don't deserve that.

After the debate, an online NBC News/Survey Monkey poll

found that 27 percent of likely women voters said the debate had made them think worse of Trump, despite the fact that few viewers had heard of Alicia Machado or knew what incident Hillary was referring to. That was to change by morning, as a new, perfectly timed ad from Hillary's campaign told us the whole story of how Trump, then executive producer of the Miss Universe pageant, had called Machado "Miss Piggy" and "an eating machine" after she gained what he called "massive amounts of weight" (actually fifteen pounds) during her tenure as Miss Universe. In the ad, Machado, besides detailing Trump's fat-shaming response to her weight gain, also mentioned a five-year-long struggle with an unspecified eating disorder, and described how Trump had put her issues with weight on display in a video feature of her exercising at a gym.

Trump's response was to double down: "She was the winner and she gained a massive amount of weight, and it was a real problem." He tweeted that Machado was "disgusting" and accused her of having a sex tape. And before long, the Associated Press was reporting that "Having drawn closer to Mrs. Clinton in the polls, Mr. Trump now faces an intensified clash over his personal temperament and his attitudes toward women and minorities—areas of grave concern for many voters that were at the center of the candidates' confrontation [at the debate] on Monday."

Women may be divided over reproductive rights, but weight and body-image issues transcend ideological differences. As I wrote in "Trump's Fat Phobia is a Global Issue":

Pageant winners and models are just at the extreme end of a continuum that nearly all girls and women occupy. Culturally instructed to find defect in ones body, body shaming (by parents, partners, product and fashion advertisements, how-to articles, stories of celebrity success shedding weight—need I go on?) is as much a condition of women's lives as the menstrual cycle (which Trump also wrinkled his nose at).

My piece was hardly the only one to see Trump as having dealt himself a losing woman card. "Women Won't Elect a Fat-Shamer-in-Chief" was the headline of a *Huffington Post* piece by Laura Bassett that not only detailed Trump's remarks about Machado (and Kim Kardashian and Rosie O'Donnell) but also recalled Ivana Trump's distress when her husband began an affair with model Marla Maples, telling Ivana he couldn't be sexually attracted to her anymore because her body was that of a woman who had had children. (Ivana had two cosmetic surgeries, but to no avail.)

Trump was in trouble. And it only got worse just a bit over a week later, when the 2005 *Access Hollywood* tapes broke. At first, to my amazement, MSNBC announced their release as just another "problem" for Trump's "gender gap" (while continuing to report the drip of Hillary's emails as potentially fatal). But they had underestimated not only the outrage of women, but also the GOP's horror at having their nominee revealed to be such an enemy of "family values." This was their signature, their trademark! And now a hot mic had revealed not merely that the newly married Trump had had extramarital affairs—that was a glass house few politicians could stand in—but had boasted that "when you're a star" you can do anything you want to women:

I'm automatically attracted to beautiful women—I just start kissing them, it's like a magnet. Just kiss. I don't even wait. And when you're a star, they let you do it. You can do anything. Grab 'em by the pussy.

Earlier in the conversation, Trump recalls trying to put the moves on a married woman:

> . . . I failed. I'll admit it. I did try to fuck her, she was married . . . and I moved on her very heavily. I took her out furniture shopping. She wanted to get some furniture and I told her "I'll show you where you can get some nice furniture." I moved on her like a bitch, and I could not get there, and she was married. And all the sudden I see her and she's got the big phony tits, she's totally changed her look.

In a prepared statement, Trump responded to the clip: "This was locker-room banter, a private conversation that took place many years ago. Bill Clinton has said far worse to me on the golf course—not even close. I apologize if anyone was offended." I doubt that he was expecting the massive GOP distancing that followed. Paul Ryan said he was "sickened" by Trump's remarks. Mitch McConnell invoked his three daughters and described Trump's comments as showing an "utter lack of respect for women." RNC chairman Reince Priebus said "No woman should ever be described in these terms or talked about in this manner. Ever." Governor Gary Herbert of Utah: "beyond offensive and despicable." Mitt Romney: "Such vile degradations demean our wives and daughters and corrupt America's face to the world."

After Trump was elected, the *Access Hollywood* tape slid down the same rabbit hole where all the "Never Trump" complaints had disappeared. But when the tapes first came out, there was a general sense that his abuses had finally "gone too far." Within days, Hillary's numbers were climbing to a significant lead, and Michelle Obama had delivered a gripping speech in which she described Trump's behavior as having "shaken me to my core in a way I could not have predicted." There was GOP talk of reversing the ticket, and putting Pence at the top. Chuck Todd speculated that Trump might not even show up for the next debate.

But Trump had other ideas in mind. "I've said some foolish things," he admitted, on a video posted to his Facebook page, "but there's a big difference between the words and actions of other people. Bill Clinton has actually abused women, and Hillary has bullied, attacked, shamed, and intimidated his victims. We will discuss this more in the coming days. See you at the debate on Sunday."

Throughout the election, Trump had been threatening to bring Bill's sexual troubles back onto center stage if Hillary wasn't "nice" to him. (We now have a president who has the vocabulary and emotional range of a five year old.) Now, true to his promise and clearly finished with being "nice," ninety minutes before the October 9 debate, Trump staged a media event with three women who decades ago had accused Bill Clinton of sexual misconduct and one woman who was twelve when Hillary Clinton was the court-appointed defender for the man who raped her. Trump also invited them into the debate hall as his guests; they sat in a row, portending of ominous accusations to come during the debate, while television cameras flipped back and forth between them and the row occupied by Bill and Chelsea.

It was a reality-TV event, highly orchestrated and of no relevance to Hillary's fitness for the presidency. Unless you are prepared to argue that Hillary ought to have quit her job when assigned a rapist to defend—in which case the very concept of a court-appointed public defender goes out the window—that charge against her is pretty flimsy. As for the other accusations, they went to Bill's behavior, not Hillary's, and the circumstances surrounding them are far from clear, largely because the women involved were so shamelessly exploited by the right wing. The Paula Jones case, which had been pursued by Ken Starr in order to entrap Clinton into lying about his affair with Monica Lewinsky, was dismissed by judge Susan Webber Wright. Juanita Broaddrick, in a sworn affidavit, denied the claim made by Jones's legal team that Clinton had invited her to a hotel room and forced her to have sex; under oath, Broaddrick said the rumors were "unfounded" and "untrue." My inclination is always to take women's charges of abuse seriously, but when political machinations are involved, facts become murkier. I have no idea what Bill Clinton did or didn't do with Jones or Broaddrick, but what is clear is that both women were used by his enemies for political purposes. Gennifer Flowers was a consensual affair which took place before Clinton was elected to the presidency. Conspicuously missing from the audience was Monica Lewinsky, who has steadfastly insisted that there was nothing abusive (or even disrespectful) about Bill Clinton's behavior. She maintained this even when the FBI was threatening her with a twenty-seven-year-long prison sentence.

Anderson Cooper, early in the debate, brought up the subject of the *Access Hollywood* tapes, and Trump reminded us, once again, that: "If you look at Bill Clinton, far worse. Mine are words and his was action. What he's done to women, there's never been anybody in the history of politics in this nation who's been so abusive to women." Trump's assumption that words are always more "innocent" than "action" shows his lack of understanding of just what was so abusive—what it was that shook Michelle Obama "to [her] core"—about what he said to Billy Bush. Bill Clinton (along with many other males in positions of power) has had extramarital affairs that were shielded from exposure. But there's nothing to suggest he thinks of women as trophies or his for the taking, and much to suggest exactly the opposite. It's clear, from Monica as well as Hillary, that he's drawn to women with brains and strong personalities, and despite Trump's claim that he has heard "far worse" from Bill while golfing with him, it's difficult to imagine the Bill Clinton that Monica Lewinsky writes about bragging about women letting him do whatever he wants with them.

To my mind, what was so revolting about the *Access Hollywood* conversation was not that Trump had extramarital sex, or even that he bragged about his "conquests," but that he did so with such utter disdain, such contempt, for the women whose "pussies" he grabbed, with their "big, phony tits" and readiness to "do anything" for a star. It was that attitude that sent many women casting early votes for Clinton: "I didn't vote for her because she's a woman," as a sixty-six-year-old retired teacher in Arizona said, "I vote for her because as a person who has been in a domestic violence situation, Donald Trump scares the livin' bejeebers out of me."

As is probably obvious by now, I'm not very receptive to revelations about private sexual behavior. But I have to admit that I cheered when Anderson Cooper, repeatedly questioning Trump as to whether he had done any of the things he bragged about on the tape, finally got an explicit denial from

Trump. The "No, I didn't" was sandwiched in hurriedly between two other points, and it was obvious that Trump knew
he was lying and would probably get himself in trouble with
it.

He did. Within days several women had come forward,
and ultimately a dozen women—journalists, beauty contest-
ents, receptionists—alleged that Trump kissed and groped
them against their will. Machado was an insult, and the
Access Hollywood tapes were revolting, but this was alleged
assault—a trauma with which one in six American women has
had a personal experience. One in three has been sexually harassed at work. These numbers, presumably, are indifferent
with respect to political affiliation—and millions of women
could relate. By late October, the allegations were well on
their way to creating what might have become a bipartisan
coalition of female voters against Trump, with eight million
women responding to a tweet asking them to describe their
personal experiences with sexual assault. Several public fig-
ures told their stories, too, on television.

It seemed at that moment as though, despite the emails,
the Clinton Foundation, the GOP hate-mongering, the media's exaggeration of every "scandal" and Sanders's splitting
of the democratic ranks, Trump was about to be decisively
vanquished. The polls were all strongly predicting it. A Clinton victory seemed, for the first time in months, a virtual inevitability.

That wasn't to be.

7.

Coup d'État

The "Other" Email Scandal

On October 4, right before the *Access Hollywood* tapes broke, an article appeared in *The Washington Post*, describing the disappointment of Roger Stone and other backers of Donald Trump that the anti-secrecy organization WikiLeaks had not yet produced the "October surprise" it had been promising. "For weeks," the article read, the Trump contingent had "hyped the tantalizing possibility" that a set of documents would be released that would "doom Hillary Clinton's chances in November."

In July, WikiLeaks had stirred up internal trouble among the Democrats, renewing the anger of Bernie supporters by releasing emails containing snipes against Sanders by members of the DNC. Bernie himself didn't find the comments shocking. "If they went into our emails," he said, "I'm sure there would be statements that would be less than flattering about, you know, the Clinton staff. That's what happens in campaigns." But his supporters weren't as sanguine, and complained loudly that the emails confirmed their suspicions that the primary had been "rigged."

The promised October leaks, whose origin Julian Assange

would not reveal, were touted to be "historic," and Texas radio host Alex Jones pronounced that "the Clintons will be devastated." Assange recommended patience; he promised to reveal documents every week for the following ten weeks, and said that "some will have a direct bearing on the U.S. election."

We now know, thanks to a fourteen-page U.S. intelligence finding released on January 6, 2017—a joint product of the CIA, FBI, and National Security Agency—that the leaks were part of an intelligence operation personally ordered by Vladimir Putin with the purpose of "denying Hillary Clinton the presidency" and "installing Donald Trump in the Oval Office." Putin had held a grudge against Clinton since 2011, the report stated, blaming her for inciting mass protests against his regime. As described by *The New York Times*, who devoted a massively headlined first page to the news, the "classified, damning report," "a virtually unheard-of, real-time revelation by the American intelligence agencies that undermined the legitimacy of the president who is about to direct them—made the case that Mr. Trump was the favored candidate of Mr. Putin," whose efforts to "undermine [Clinton's] future presidency" intensified when she appeared more likely to win the election. In addition to the email drip, Russian intelligence also used state-funded broadcasts, third-party intermediaries, and paid social media trolls to spread false information "discrediting Secretary Clinton and publicly contrasting her unfavorably to [Trump]."

How destructive to Clinton were the leaks? The report, unsurprisingly, was unable to officially make an assessment of that, as it would require sophisticated multifactorial analysis of events, polls, and public opinion leading up to the election to determine. Trump, of course, insists that they had absolutely no effect on the election results, and most pundits have seemed happy to go along with that conclusion. (Trump also described the focus on the hacks as a "witch hunt" conducted against him—pretty ironic, considering the hacks themselves were part of a witch hunt aimed at the Clintons.) Common sense, however, leads in a different direction than the "no effect" conclusion. If the leaks were so innocuous, why then did Trump's campaign and GOP-friendly media invest so much in disseminating the information contained in them? And how to explain why the right-wing media had initially bragged about how "devastating" they were going to be? Were they just teasing? Or did they know more than they revealed at the time?

On this, the "middle-of-the-road" news stations like CNN shy away from what they fear might be seen as partisan, speculative analysis (although they actually engage in it all the time). But I don't have the same anxiety—and I encourage readers of this book to consider the absurdity of imagining that a concerted Russian campaign of anti-Clinton propaganda—especially when put in the context of the other anti-Clinton tactics and atmospherics described in this book—had no effect on the outcome of the election. By themselves, it's unlikely that the leaks were a deciding factor. But the leaks never operated "by themselves." For one thing, being dropped like fresh chum (as Gabriel Debenedetti put it) in the media water regularly, they prevented other news from grabbing reporters' attention. And then, too, their content—although relatively insignificant—was well employed to discredit Hillary at every turn, contributing to the perfect storm of Hillary hate (or at the very least, mistrust) that helped carry Trump to the White House.

Bernie Sanders's fans, for example, who regarded

WikiLeaks as part of the "left," had, as I've mentioned, seized on email evidence that the DNC had favored Clinton and "rigged" the primary, diluting whatever enthusiasm for Clinton had been developing among them—and in many cases, solidifying their determination to stay away from the polls, a failure of turnout that Nate Silver has calculated was deadly to Clinton's chances of winning. The right probably didn't need to be convinced, but nonetheless gobbled up and publicized any new examples of Clinton's "duplicity"—such as when leaked emails revealed comments in which she had defended the notion that one's public position often must diverge from one's private ideas. (I found this a particularly unfair attack. The fact is, if all of us, all the time, publicly expressed what we are privately thinking, there would be few friends or colleagues left standing.

Arguably most destructive, though, because of the timing, were the leaks about the Clinton Foundation. The suspect items consisted almost entirely of emails in which Chelsea Clinton expressed concerns that large donations given during the time Hillary was secretary of state might be seen as involving "pay for play"—favoritism for those governments and businesses who were big benefactors. There was no evidence of such "pay for play" in the emails, just concerns about "optics." When the emails were leaked, however, the Foundation was already a right-wing hot button because of the publication, in May 2015, of *Clinton Cash*, written by Peter Schweizer, *Breitbart* editor at large and president of the Government Accountability Institute (co-founded by Steve Bannon, who was Trump's campaign manager and is now his right-hand man). *Clinton Cash* was full of rhetorical speculation but no evidence. After sixteen months of news investigations into the Foundation, nothing nefarious had been unearthed.

Lack of evidence, however, has never dampened the enthusiasm of Clinton's enemies, among whom the book became a kind of contemporary cult classic. Most dangerously, *Clinton Cash* provided grist for the mill of a "rogue," viciously anti-Clinton New York faction within the FBI, who made the investigation into the foundation "very high priority," despite skepticism from FBI headquarters and superiors at the Justice Department. The rogue agents used *Clinton Cash* (in author Schweizer's own words) as a "road map" for their investigations, while the leaked emails brought a fresh wave of suspicion about the Clinton Foundation to the forefront of public attention. The Trump campaign, Fox News, *Morning Joe*, and others declared outrage over "blurred lines between the Clinton Foundation and the family's business interests." (Trump should talk!) Even a responsible academic like Princeton's Eddie Glaude, without a shred of evidence beyond "bad optics," fulminated on *Morning Joe* about Clinton's serious "moral and ethical deficit."

Note well the timing of all this. On October 17, in the wake of the *Access Hollywood* tapes and Michelle Obama's gripping speech, Nate Silver's "election update" reported that with three weeks to go, Hillary Clinton had a "significant lead" of 6–7 points and an 86 percent chance of winning the election.

On October 27, the headlines exploded with news of the WikiLeaks emails concerning the Clinton Foundation. Someone was clearly watching—Putin or Assange—and knew exactly what he was doing.

James Comey's Abuse of Power, act 2

James Comey, for reasons that are still not clear, had already gone way beyond FBI protocol, and according to many committed a gross abuse of his own power, when, in early July, he had described Clinton's handling of emails as "careless."

He also revealed a shifting set of scruples about what the public has a right to know, displaying no obligation to publicly correct the record on Clinton's "carelessness" when Elijah Cummings and Matt Cartwright pressed him to admit that Clinton had not acted carelessly (and by implication, not lied) in treating unmarked emails as unclassified.

Yet, on October 28 he compounded his earlier actions and ignored the Justice Department's guidelines barring the release of information about ongoing investigations—or even returning indictments—involving individuals running for office in close proximity (within sixty days) to an election, and sent a letter to Congress saying that "in connection with an unrelated case, the FBI has learned of the existence of emails that appear to be pertinent to the investigation." These emails, discovered on the laptop of Anthony Weiner, former congressman and husband of Clinton's aide and confidant Huma Abedin, needed to be reviewed to "determine whether they contained classified information, as well as to assess their importance to the investigation."

Comey's motives for this extraordinary additional breach of protocol remain unclear. E. J. Dionne, in *The Washington Post*, suggests that he was intimidated by pressure from congressional Republicans who'd been furious about his earlier exoneration of Clinton, or perhaps (or also) by factions within the FBI who had been "complaining privately that

Comey should have tried harder to make a case" against Clinton. Comey's subordinates anonymously told reporters that felt felt obligated to "update Congress" on his earlier (equally irregular) report.

Whatever Comey's motives, the slime factor went beyond his actions. As Rudy Giuliani's undisciplined blabbing revealed, Trump campaign officials actually knew Comey's letter to Congress was coming beforehand, and made the most of it: "I think [Trump's] got a surprise or two that you're going to hear about in the next few days . . . a couple of things that should turn this around," Giuliani told Fox the day before Comey's letter to Congress surfaced; he also couldn't resist bragging that he had insider knowledge of "a kind of revolution going on inside the FBI" springing from tensions between those who supported Comey's legal exoneration of Clinton and those—the same New York faction for whom *Clinton Cash* was a bible—who were out for more blood. As E. J. Dionne had suggested, it's likely that Comey's hand was forced by this faction, either in collusion with Giuliani or simply out of their own hatred for Clinton. What is clear, though—unless Giuliani was just making the whole thing up, and why should he have?—is that, as Steven Rosenfeld wrote in Alternet, there was "a cadre of Hillary-hating agents that pushed the Bureau to interfere in the 2016 election in a manner that can only be described as an attempted coup."

Does that language sound too conspiratorial to you? Before the campaign I might have thought so, but the confluence, in the weeks before the election, of "a disastrous series of unfortunate events" for Hillary suggests that talk of a "coup," although somewhat metaphorical, is not an exaggeration. For although these events were not orchestrated by one evil genius or agency, they may as well have been.

Consider, once again, the timing:

It's eleven days before the election, Clinton has three successful debates behind her, Trump's nasty behavior with women is on garish display, and the polls are looking really good for Hillary. Then, "FBI says emails found in Anthony Weiner's sexting scandal may have links to Clinton inquiry" (the headline in the *Los Angeles Times*).

"May have links" is broad and vacuous; in fact, at the time of the announcement, all that the FBI could report was the "appearance" of "pertinence." (They hadn't even gotten a warrant as yet to determine the content of the emails, and could not "predict how long it will take us to complete this additional work.") "Sexting scandal" was irrelevant ("Weiner's emails" would have been sufficient), but did a great job of reminding readers of the sleaze factor among the Clinton men. Ironically, Trump had just been accused of sexual assault by twelve different women—and until Comey's announcement, it was looking like it might sink him. But now, the damned emails were front and center again, and both the GOP and the media treated the news as explosive. MSNBC's Kristen Welker declared that the "full enormity" of this new information could "up-end the entire election." And Donald Trump, at the opening of a campaign rally in New Hampshire, made the most of Comey's announcement: "Hillary Clinton's corruption is on a scale we have never seen before. We must not let her take her criminal scheme into the Oval Office." Referring to Comey's original exoneration, he applauded the FBI for revisiting the case: "This was a grave miscarriage of justice that the American people fully understood. Perhaps finally justice will be done."

The FBI's conclusion was not what Trump intimated it

would be. As Clinton's campaign had suspected was the case, the emails were revealed to be duplicates of those already scrutinized and found entirely innocent by the FBI.

By then, however, the election was just two days away, and the damage was done.

Epilogue

Epilogue

How harmful to Clinton was the second Comey intervention? Common sense alone suggests that the revival of "the email scandal," which had led so many Americans to see Clinton as untrustworthy and a liar, would have had a significant effect. Before the "new" email investigation was announced, the national consciousness was awash with revulsion and condemnation of Trump over the *Access Hollywood* tapes and the allegations that followed. After Comey's letter? For all intents and purposes it was as though the *Access Hollywood* tapes had never happened, and the twelve women alleging abuse had never come forward. "Breaking News" of "new email revelations" swept all that away.

Since the inauguration, however, things have changed. With Trump in the White House, all hope of a "pivot" is gone, and we now know that the man we elected is just what he seemed to be, and worse: an inveterate liar and authoritarian narcissist who appears to take what few orders he obeys not from constitutional constraints on his authority, but from right-wing ideologues like Steve Bannon and the interests of big business. In November, after the election, we were all instructed to have an "open mind" and "give him a chance." But the abusive tweets never stopped and the bald-faced lies—about the size of the crowds at his inauguration, the three million "fraudulent" votes for Clinton, the failure of the "dishonest" press to cover terrorist attacks—have become daily fare. At the same time, we've found out that candidate Trump *didn't* lie about the things many of us most feared: in his first few weeks he ordered frantic, if clumsy, assaults on Obamacare, environmental and consumer protection, reproductive rights, and as of this writing, is attempting to put into effect the ban on Muslim immigration he promised throughout his campaign.

In the face of what seems to be a full-scale Trumpian attack on democracy, the rule of law, and the authority of fact, that Clinton was ever seen by any liberal or left-leaning voters as "the lesser of two evils" is painfully surreal, and those polls that showed that people found Trump more "trustworthy" now seem a betrayal of reason, evidence of just how deeply we were conned—not only by Trump but by the popular narratives concocted by the GOP and perpetuated by the media.

The GOP and news commentators alike cried "sore loser" when the Clinton campaign claimed Comey's interference had cost them the election. We now know, however, that the Clinton campaign's interpretation is highly likely to be correct. The polls, we were often told, simply got it wrong in predicting Clinton would be the winner. As Vox points out, however, "much of what pundits are describing as error . . . might better be described as the 'Comey effect.'" For very few of those polls were taken after Comey "re-opened" the investigation, which also happened to coincide with the final stretch of days when an "unusually large number of undecided voters" were making up their minds. Many of those late-deciding voters were likely to have had lingering reservations about Clinton (otherwise, why were they undecided?), but we know from earlier polls that such reservations were almost always based on mistrust, issuing largely from the faux "email scandal"— *which had just been revived by James Comey.*

Comparison of absentee votes and votes on Election Day show evidence of a late surge toward Trump. Bolstering the "Comey effect" hypothesis, too, is the fact that the national polls show indisputable evidence that Clinton's margin over Trump fell swiftly and steeply directly after the Comey letter—and never recovered. By November 3, Clinton's lead in the national polls was evaporating, and Trump had several plausible electoral map routes to victory.

That "Comey was a massive blow to Clinton at a pivotal moment in the election" seems beyond doubt.[12] But if this book has argued anything at all, it's that Hillary's loss wasn't "just" the result of Comey's interference, or "just" the result of Putin's hacks, or GOP witch hunts, or fake news, or right-wing Hillary hate books. Her defeat isn't "just" attributable to "sexism" or "just" the fault of the media. It wasn't "just" caused by the "Sanders effect," which splintered democratic unity by generation. The destruction of Hillary Clinton's candidacy—and our hope of defeating Donald Trump—was the

[12] Comey's duplicity concerning what the public should and shouldn't be told has finally begun to be exposed. More and more evidence has come to light that an FBI investigation into Trump campaign connections with Russia has indeed been underway for some time. Yet, in a recent Senate hearing, Comey refused to say whether or not there was such an investigation, citing the protocol of not commenting on investigations in an open forum! Maine's Angus King (an independent) was having none of it. "The irony of your making that statement, I cannot avoid," he said. Adam Schiff, top Democrat on the House Intelligence Committee, later told ABC News: "I think there's been a profound question raised as to whether Director Comey is dealing in an even-handed manner with the investigation of the Clinton emails and any investigation that may or may not be happening with respect to the Trump campaign."

result of *all* of these. One on top of the other, overlapping, mutually reinforcing, a massive pile-on of open assaults, secret strategies, unconscious biases, and blundering media business as usual simply proved too much. Even so, Hillary Clinton won nearly three million more votes than Trump. As to those states she lost: she didn't "fail" to deliver, as it's now often described. I would say instead that she almost made it, despite a daily barrage of character attacks, lies, and distortions.

When I began this epilogue, it was the day after Donald Trump's inauguration, and millions of women, men, and children were gathering around the world to protest his policies. "Where was all this energy before the election?" one newscaster asked. Undoubtedly, many of the protestors had voted for Hillary Clinton. But the newscaster has a point. If the same coalition of anti-Trump forces, united not by a single issue or a single preferred candidate, had put their hearts and minds together with the aim of defeating him, it surely would have been accomplished. As things actually went, however, fear of a Trump presidency was not motivation enough to generate mass enthusiasm for the one action that was required to defeat him: electing Hillary Clinton.

Many people, to be sure, simply couldn't wrap their minds around the possibility that Trump could actually win, and didn't vote for Hillary, thinking she had it sewn up—as the pre-Comey polls had predicted. But others didn't want to vote for Hillary and couldn't bring themselves to, because they had been schooled in and accepted a false picture of who she is. We've seen, throughout this book, how and by whom that false picture was created—and how it was greatly enhanced by the (seemingly non-partisan) mainstream media, who served as a conveyor belt and mass disseminator of negative narratives and imagery about Hillary.

The forces working against Clinton, then, were multiple and determined—and as it turned out, as effective as any true conspiracy in creating a critical mass of voters to derail her campaign. Who belonged to that mass? Of course, there were the "natural" Trump lovers, the racists and xenophobes who were with him from the beginning. There were the faithful Republicans who wouldn't vote for a Democrat under any circumstances. And there were those who wouldn't vote for a woman—any woman—no matter how qualified or experienced she was. Trump would have gotten all those votes in any case.

The voters I have in mind are different. They belong, mostly, to the almost five million Obama voters who either didn't vote at all, voted third party, or may even have voted for Trump: The white, middle-class, suburban women who wanted to distance themselves from the unscrupulous, cold, "elitist" politician who was definitely not their kind of woman. The rust belt men who believed she was the "corporate whore" who had proposed putting coal miners out of business (rather than—as was actually the case—an honest candidate describing an economic reality that had to be confronted by the government whose responsibility it was to find other means of employment for them). The Sanders fans who came to see Hillary as barely better than Trump, and who just couldn't rouse themselves to campaign for her (or for too many, to vote for her). The 46 percent of black voters under the age of thirty who did not vote, who may or may not have been Sanders supporters but who often, when asked why they didn't intend on voting for Hillary, recited the Sanders caricature.

The many hardworking, stressed, perfectly decent folks with little spare time to research the facts, who put their trust in the media to tell them what was important, what was true, what to believe, and who came to believe that Hillary Clinton was too "untrustworthy" to be our president. The man I met at the grocery store who crossed Hillary off his list when she seemed to be describing many of his relatives as "a basket of deplorables."

That man hadn't heard, of course, what Hillary went on to say (which was not widely reported by the mainstream media), that the other half of Trump voters:

> are people who feel that government has let them down, the economy has let them down, nobody cares about them, nobody worries about what happens to their lives and their futures. They are just desperate for change. Doesn't really even matter where it comes from. They won't wake up and see their jobs disappear, lose a kid to heroin, feel like they're in a dead end. Those are people who we have to understand and empathize with as well.

That man cast his vote against someone with her name, but it wasn't Hillary Clinton.

Sources Consulted and Cited

Sources Consulted and Cited

Preface

Allen, Jonathan and Parnes, Amie, *HRC*, N.Y.: Random House, 2014.

American Rhetoric, "Top 100 Speeches," http://www.americanrhetoric.com/top100speechesall.html

"Behind Trump's victory: Divisions by race, gender, education," Pew Research Center, November 9, 2016

Bordo, Susan, *The Creation of Anne Boleyn*, N.Y.: Houghton Mifflin Harcourt, 2013.

Castillo, Walbert, "How we voted-by age, education, race and sexual orientation," *USA Today,* November 9, 2016.

Chozick, Amy, "Mothers of Black Victims Emerge as a Force for Hillary Clinton," *The New York Times*, April 13, 2016. https://nyti.ms/1goblen

Clinton, Hillary, *Living History*, New York: Simon and Schuster, 2003.

Davis, Rachaell, "Polling Results Estimate 94 percent of Black Women Voters Chose Hillary Clinton, *Essence,* November 9, 2016. http://www.essence.com/news/politics/most-black-women-voted-for-hillary-clinton

Draper, Robert, "How Hillary Became 'Hillary'," *The New York Times Magazine*, October 11, 2016. www.nytimes.com/2016/10/16/magazine/how-hillary-clinton-became-hillary.html?_r=0S

Friedan, Betty, *The Feminine Mystique*, N.Y.: WW Norton, 1963.

Gates, Henry Louis, "Hating Hillary," *The New Yorker,* February 26, 1996.

Howard, Jason, "A rural man grieves Hillary Clinton's defeat: Her strength gave hope to outsiders like me." *Salon,* November 14, 2016. www.salon.com/2016/11/15/a-rural-man-grieves-hillary-clintons-defeat-her-success-gave-hope-to-outsiders-like-me/.

Kruse, Michael, "My Country Accepts Me as a Woman," Politico, July 1, 2016. http://www.politico.com/magazine/story /2016/07/hillary-clinton-2016-transgender-rights-passport-policy-state-department-lgbt-equality-214007

Lucey, Catherine, "Black Women Uniting in Support for Clinton in 2016," *PBS Newshour,* March 26, 2016.

McEwan, Melissa, "Why older women are so enthusiastic about Hillary Clinton," Shareblue, September 29, 2016. http://shareblue.com/why-older-women-are-so-enthusiastic-about-hillary-clinton/

Younge, Gary, "Seven Ages of Hillary Clinton: a woman who in her time has played many parts," *The Guardian*, January 30, 2016.

Introduction

Bordo, Susan, "The Creation of 'Hillary Clinton' and the Deconstruction of Hillary Clinton." *Die Zeit Online,* November 19, 2016. www.zeit.de/kultur/2016-11/hillary-clinton-image-deconstruction-susan-bordo.

Bordo, Susan, "How To Try a Witch in the 21st Century." *Huffington Post,* June 20, 2016. www.huffingtonpost.com /susan-bordo-/how-to-try-a-witch-in-the_b_11074178. html.

Cohn, Nate, "Why Trump Had an Edge in the Electoral College." December 19, 2016. www.nytimes.com/2016/12/19 /upshot/why-trump-had-an-edge-in-the-electoral-college.html.

Collins, Eliza, "Sanders: Not enough to say, 'I'm a woman,

vote for me." *USA Today,* November 21, 2016. www.us-
atoday.com/story/news/politics/onpolitics/2016/11/21
/sanders-identity-politics/94221972/.

Dovere, Edward-Isaac, "How Clinton lost Michigan—and
blew the election." Politico, December 14, 2016. www
.politico.com/story/2016/12/michigan-hillary-clin-
ton-trump-232547.

Dovere, Edward-Isaac, "Inside the Loss Clinton Saw Coming."
Politico, November 9, 2016. www.politico.com/magazine
/story/2016/11/hillary-clinton-loses-2016-election-
214439.

Eichenwald, Kurt, "The Myths Democrats Swallowed That
Cost Them the Presidential Election." *Newsweek,* November 14, 2016. www.newsweek.com/myths-cost-dem-
ocrats-presidential-election-521044.

Post-election panel with Chris Matthews, MSNBC, November 8, 2016. http://www.msnbc.com/hardball.

Ioffe, Julia, "Apocalypse Now: Survivalists Dig in for November 9." Politico, November 8, 2016. www.politico.com
/magazine/story/2016/11/hillary-clinton-donald-trump-
2016-preppers-214433.

Jamieson, Amber and Gabbat, Adam, "'You don't fit the
image': Hillary Clinton's decades-long push against a
sexist press." *The Guardian,* September 15, 2016. https:
//www.theguardian.com/us-news/2016/sep/15/hil-
lary-clinton-press-sexism-media-interviews.

Johnson, Marcus H., "Stop Calling It Identity Politics—Its
Civil Rights." *Extra Newsfeed,* November 22, 2016. www
.extranewsfeed.com/stop-calling-it-identity-politics-its-
civil-rights-50ef9bdfda09#.iuvspc0ig.

Klein, Ezra, "Why the Clinton America sees isn't the Clinton colleagues know." Vox., July 11, 2016. http://www
.vox.com/a/hillary-clinton-interview/the-gap-listen-
er-leadership-quality.

McCaskill, Nolan and Nelson, Louis, Politico, November 2016.
http://www.politico.com/story/2016/11/trump-clin-
ton-investigation-kellyanne-conway-231735.

Merica, Dan, "Sanders supporters shower Clinton motor-

cade with dollar bills." CNN, April 17, 2016. http://cnn.it
/20Mmdjj.

Morse, Brandon, "Bernie Sanders explains why anti-political
correctness helped win Trump the election." TheBlaze,
December 13, 2016. http://www.theblaze.com/news/2016
/12/13/bernie-sanders-explains-why-anti-political-cor-
rectness-helped-win-trump-the-election/.

"MSNBC Live" November 12, 2016

Nguyen, Tina, "Ben Carson Goes Rogue, Links Hillary Clinton to Lucifer." *Vanity Fair*, July 19, 2016. http://www
.vanityfair.com/news/2016/07/ben-carson-rnc-conven-
tion-lucifer.

Reilly, Katie, "Read Chris Christie's Convention Speech Attacking Hillary Clinton." *Time*, July 22, 2016. http://time
.com/4419974/chris-christie-republican-conven-
tion-speech/.

Smith, Allen, "What Went Down at the Republican National
Convention." *Business Insider,* July 26, 2016. http://www
.businessinsider.com/republican-national-convention-re-
cap-2016-7.

Wilhelm, Heather, "Reminder: Hillary Clinton Lost Because
She's Hillary Clinton." *The National Review,* November
11, 2016. Accessed January 25, 2017. www.nationalreview
.com/article/442063/hillary-clinton-lost-because-shes-
hillary-clinton.

1. Dilemmas of the Female Politician

Allen, Jonathan and Parnes, Amie, *HRC*, N.Y.:Random House,
2014.

Auerbach, Lauren, "Report: Mauren Dowd frequently Uses
Gender to Mock Democrats." Alternet, June 10, 2008.

http://www.alternet.org/story/87666/report%3A_mau-reen_dowd_repeatedly_uses_gender_to_mock_demo-crats.

Barron, John, "Is Hillary Clinton 'likable' enough?" ABC News Australia, September 2, 2015. http://www.abc.net.au/news/2015-09-03/barron-is-hillary-clinton-likeable-enough/6743836Ric.

Bernstein, Carl, *A Woman in Charge,* N.Y.: Random House, 2007.

Brownmiller, Susan, *In Our Time: Memoir of a Revolution,* N.Y.: Delta, 1999.

Clinton, Hillary, *Living History,* New York: Simon and Schuster, 2003.

Cohen, Richard, "'You're Likable Enough' Costs Obama." RealClearPolitics, January 10, 2008. http://www.realclearpolitics.com/articles/2008/01/youre_likable_enough_costs_oba.html.

Cramer, Ruby, "Hillary Clinton wants to talk to you about love and kindness." BuzzFeed, January 25, 2016. www.buzzfeed.com/rubycramer/hillary-clinton-wants-to-talk-to-you-about-love-and-kindness?utm_term=.poxG7KjGa1.

Doyle, Sady, "America loves women like Hillary Clinton—as long as they're not asking for a promotion." *Quartz,* February 25, 2016. www.qz.com/624346/america-loves-women-like-hillary-clinton-as-long-as-theyre-not-asking-for-a-promotion/.

Dowd, Maureen, "Candidate's Wife; Hillary Clinton as Aspiring First Lady: Role Model, or a 'Hall Monitor' Type." *The New York Times,* May 18, 1992. http://www.nytimes.com/1992/05/18/us/1992-campaign-candidate-s-wife-hillary-clinton-aspiring-first-lady-role-model.html?pagewanted=all.

Dowd, Maureen, "A Wake-Up Call for Hillary." *The New York Times,* March 2, 2008. http://www.nytimes.com/2008/03/02|/opinion/02dowd.html

Dowd, Maureen, "Shake, Rattle and Roll." *The New York Times,* November 18, 2007. http://www.nytimes.com/2007/11/18/opinion/18dowd.html

Draper, Robert, "How Hillary Became 'Hillary'." *The New York Times Magazine,* October 11, 2016. www.nytimes.com /2016/10/16/magazine/how-hillary-clinton-became-hillary.html?_r=0.

D'Souza, Dinesh, *Hillary's America,* N.J.: Regnery, 2016.

Eleveld, Kerry, "Hillary Clinton's excellent answer on the 'trust' issue: people trust her when she's doing the job." *Daily Kos,* August 5, 2016. www.dailykos.com/story /2016/8/5/1557214/-Hillary-Clinton-s-excellent-answer-on-the-trust-issue-people-trust-her-when-she-s-doing-the-job.

Evans, Sara, *Personal Politics,* N.Y.: Vintage, 1980.

Freedman, Estelle, *No Turning Back: The History of Feminism and the Future of Women,* N.Y.: Ballantine, 2002.

Gilbert, Matthew, "We've seen Donald Trump's theatrics before—on reality TV." *Globe,* August 25, 2015.

"Hillary Clinton 1992 Interview on the *Today* Show," https: //youtu.be/-namImCszCk.

Kelly, Michael, "Saint Hillary," *The New York Times,* May 23, 1993. http://www.nytimes.com/1993/05/23/magazine/saint-hillary.html?pagewanted=all.

Kenney, Charles, "Hillary The Wellesley Years." *The Boston Globe,* January 12, 1993. www.bostonglobe.com/news /politics/1993/01/12/hillary-the-wellesley-years /OEapzWGuzSNAFiIHL2zm9K/story.html.

Konnikova, Maria, "Lean Out: The Dangers for Women Who Negotiate." *The New Yorker,* June 10, 2014.

Morton, Andrew, *Monica's Story,* N.Y.: St. Martin's Press, 1999.

Nashrulla, Tasneem, "Women Are Totally Relating To Hillary Clinton's Explanation Of Why She Seems 'Walled Off'." BuzzFeed, September 8, 2016. www.buzzfeed.com /tasneemnashrulla/hillary-clinton-humans-of-new-york-post?utm_term=.bo3yoK8RdO#.kvVjJG4RXe.

Sandberg, Sheryl, *Lean In: Women, Work, and the Will to Lead,* N.Y: Knopf, 2013

Tamar, "'Hellish Housewife' Hillary." Daily Kos, Ocotober 1, 2007. http://www.dailykos.com/story/2007/10/1 /392609/.

Shen, Aviva, "Students see male professors as brilliant ge-
niuses, female professors as bossy and annoying." *Think-
Progress*, February 7, 2015.

Shorenstein Center on Media, Politics, and Public Policy, Harvard Kennedy School, "Research: Media Coverage of the
2016 Election." Sept 7, 2016. https://shorensteincenter
.org/research-media-coverage-2016-election/.

"Talk of the Town." *The New Yorker*, March 10, 2014.

Timpf, Katherine, "Hillary Clinton is Not a Feminist." *The
National Review*, December 30, 2015.

Traister, Rebecca, "Hillary Clinton's Campaign was Never
Going to be Easy, But Did it Have to Get This Hard?"
New York Magazine, May 30, 2016.

Daniel Wattenberg, "The Lady MacBeth of Little Rock." *The
American Spectator*, August 1992. Reprinted November 20, 2015, https://spectator.org/64728_wests-rude-
houseguests/.

2. The "Woman Card"

Abdullah, Halimah, "How women ruled the 2012 election
and where the GOP went wrong." CNN, November 8,
2012. www.cnn.com/2012/11/08/politics/women-elec-
tion/.

Associated Press, "Calif. judge says victims' bodies can
prevent rape." *CBS News*, December 13, 2012. www
.cbsnews.com/news/calif-judge-says-victims-bodies-
can-prevent-rape/.

Bassett, Laura, "House Republicans Kick Off 2014 With
Renewed Focus on Abortion, Birth Control." *Huffington
Post*, January 25, 2014. www.huffingtonpost.com/2014
/01/08/house-gop-kicks-off-2014-_n_4563303.html.

Beaumont, Thomas, "GOP in key states tries to slow anti-abortion push." CNSNews.com, August 2, 2013. www
.cnsnews.com/news/article/gop-key-states-tries-slow-
anti-abortion-push.

Bradley, Matt and Leigh, Karen, "2014 Year in Review: The Events That Shaped a Turbulent Year." *The Wall Street Journal,* December 30, 2014. www.wsj.com/articles/year-in-review-top-news-stories-of-2014-1419977543.

Clines, Francis X., "Richard Mourdock on God's Intentions."*The New York Times,* October 24, 2012. www.takingnote.blogs.nytimes.com/2012/10/24/richard-mourdock-on-gods-intentions/.

Collins, Gail, "Trump Deals the Woman Card." *The New York Times,* April 28, 2016. www.nytimes.com/2016/04/28/opinion/trump-deals-the-woman-card.html?smprod=nytcore-ipad&smid=nytcore-ipad-share.

Cosco, Joey, "Binders Full of Women is the gaffe that will never die." *The Daily Dot,* July 25, 2013. www.dailydot.com/layer8/binders-full-of-women-mitt-romney-gaffe-facebook-tumblr/.

Crockett, Emily, "Trump on *60 Minutes*: if Roe v. Wade is overturned, women will 'have to go to another state'." Vox, November 14, 2016. www.vox.com/policy-and-politics/2016/11/13/13618556/trump-60-minutes-roe-v-wade-abortion.

Culp-Ressler, Tara, "Texas Lawmaker Attempts To Block Stringent Abortion Restrictions With 13-Hour Filibuster." ThinkProgress, June 25, 2013. www.thinkprogress.org/texas-lawmaker-attempts-to-block-stringent-abortion-restrictions-with-13-hour-filibuster-afba7a8dd95a#.loxpag2zv.

Eligon, John and Schwirtz, Michael, "Senate Candidate Provokes Ire With 'Legitimate Rape' Comment." *The New York Times,* August 19, 2012. www.nytimes.com/2012/08/20/us/politics/todd-akin-provokes-ire-with-legitimate-rape-comment.html.

Gearan, Anne and Zezima, Katie, "Trump's 'woman's card' comment escalates the campaign's gender wars." *The Washington Post,* April 27, 2016. www.washingtonpost.com/politics/trumps-womans-card-comment-escalates-gender-wars-of-2016-campaign/2016/04/27

/fbe4c67a-0c2b-11e6-8ab8-9ad050f76d7d_story.html.

Graham, David A., "Why Trump Might Regret Playing 'The WomanCard' AgainstClinton." *TheAtlantic,*April27,2016. www.theatlantic.com/politics/archive/2016/04/trump-hillary-clinton-woman-card/480129/.

Hess, Amanda, "What Conservatives Taught Us About Women's Bodies in 2012." *Slate,* December 27, 2012. www.slate .com/blogs/xx_factor/2012/12/27/legitimate_rape_ rush_limbaugh_and_voting_while_menstuating_the_ most_outrageous.html.

LaFauci, Trevor, "Dear Daughter: A Letter to My Future Child in the Age of Hillary Clinton." The People's View, April 29, 2016. www.thepeoplesview.net/main/2016/4/29 /dear-daughter-a-letter-to-my-future-child-in-the-age-of-hillary-clinton#.VyX5N_Yk4WV.facebook.

Liptak, Adam, "Supreme Court Ruling Makes Same-Sex Marriage a Right Nationwide." *The New York Times,* June 26, 2015. www.nytimes.com/2015/06/27/us/supreme-court-same-sex-marriage.html.

Marcotte, Amanda, "Why did Romney Lose? Conservatives Blame Single Women." *Slate,* November 9, 2012. www.slate.com/blogs/xx_factor/2012/11/09/why_did_ romney_lose_fox_news_blames_single_women.html.

Media Matters Staff, "After Prodding By O'Reilly, Trump Floats "Overturning" *Roe V. Wade.*" MMfA, May 10, 2016. www. mediamatters.org/video/2016/05/10/after-prodding-oreilly-trump-floats-overturning-roe-v-wade/210347.

Mele, Christopher, "Medicaid Funding to End for Planned Parenthood in Texas, State Says." *The New York Times,* December 20, 2016. www.nytimes.com/2016/12/20/us/ texas-medicaid-cut-planned-parenthood-funding.html.

"'The only card she has is the woman's card': Trump on Clinton." *Reuters,* April 26, 2016. www.reuters.com/ video/2016/04/27/the-only-card-she-has-is-the-woman's-card?videoId=368276881.

Ortelpa, Olivier, "The Biggest New Events of 2015: Attack on Charlie Hebdo." *Newsweek,* December 12, 2015. www .newsweek.com/front-page-news-2015-402024.

Pollitt, Katha, "The Hillary Clinton Double Standard." *The Nation*, January 6, 2016.

Pollitt, Katha, "Why Bernie Didn't Get My Vote." *The Nation*, May 4, 2016. https://www.thenation.com/article/why-bernie-didnt-get-my-vote/.

Rappeport, Alan, "Gloria Steinem and Madeleine Albright Rebuke Young Women Backing Bernie Sanders." *The New York Times*, February 7, 2016. www.nytimes.com/2016/02/08/us/politics/gloria-steinem-madeleine-albright-hillary-clinton-bernie-sanders.html?_r=0.

Rinkunas, Susan, "The 5 Worst Decisions Mike Pence Has Made About Women's Health." *New York Magazine*, July 15, 2016.www.nymag.com/thecut/2016/07/mike-pence-abortion-womens-health-record.html.

"Sandra Fluke," *Wikipedia*.

Terkel, Amanda, "The Man Card: An American Tradition Of Presidents Using Their Gender To Get Ahead." *Huffington Post*, April 27, 2016. www.huffingtonpost.com/entry/man-card-presidents_us_5720d1a4e4b0b49df6a9bbab.

Traister, Rebecca, "Hillary Clinton vs. Herself." *New York Magazine*, May 30, 2016. www.nymag.com/daily/intelligencer/2016/05/hillary-clinton-candidacy.html?mid=fb-share-di.

Uchimiya, Ellen, "Donald Trump insults Carly Fiorina's appearance." CBS News, September 10, 2015. www.cbsnews.com/news/donald-trump-insults-carly-fiorinas-appearance/.

Weinberger, Hannah, "Where are all the millennial feminists?" *CNN*, November 10, 2012. www.cnn.com/2012/11/09/living/millennials-feminism/.

Woman Card. www.womancard.co/.

3. Bernie Sanders and the "Millennials"

Bacon, Perry, "In First Debate, Sanders Gives Clinton a Big Assist on Emails." *Meet the Press*, NBC News, October 14,

2015. http://www.nbcnews.com/meet-the-press/first-debate-sanders-gives-clinton-big-assist-emails-n444121.

Barker, Savannah, "The 1996 Article Every Millennial Should Read." *The Voidist,* April 7, 2016. https://thevoidist.com/the-1996-article-every-millennial-should-read-d9350b10e568#.ttts572id.

Baxandall, Rosalyn and Gordon, Linda, editors, *Dear Sisters,* N.Y.: Basic Books, 2000.

Bordo, Susan, "History Lesson For a Young Sanders Supporter." *Huffington Post,* February 7, 2016. www.huffingtonpost.com/susan-bordo-/history-lesson-for-a-youn_b_9168076.html.

Bradner, Eric, "Sanders: I am not 'shouting' at Hillary Clinton." CNN, October 25, 2015. www.cnn.com/2015/10/25/politics/bernie-sanders-hillary-clinton-gun-control-shouting/.

Brock, David, *Blinded by the Right,* N.Y.: Three Rivers Press, 2002.

Bump, Philip, "The Wall Street Journal's Bernie-Sanders-can-win editorial is almost entirely wrong." *The Washington Post,* May 12, 2016. www.washingtonpost.com/news/the-fix/wp/2016/05/12/the-wall-street-journals-bernie-sanders-can-win-editorial-is-almost-entirely-wrong/?utm_term=.bc2a0636da20.

Carroll, Lauren, "Hillary Clinton says she called for Wall Street regulations early in the financial crisis." Politifact, July 15, 2015. www.politifact.com/truth-o-meter/statements/2015/jul/15/hillary-clinton/hillary-clinton-says-she-called-wall-street-regula/.

Cesca, Bob, "Yes, Susan Sarandon is guilty of blind privilege: Why her comments about Trump & 'the revolution' are so wrong." *Salon,* March 30, 2016. www.salon.com/2016/03/30/yes_susan_sarandon_is_guilty_of_blind_privilege_why_her_comments_about_trump_the_revolution_are_so_wrong/.

Clinton, Hillary, *Living History,* New York: Simon and Schuster, 2003.

"First Lady Hillary Rodham Clinton's Remarks to the

Fourth Women's Conference in Beijing, China." You-Tube video, April 13, 2016. www.youtube.com/watch?v=xM4E23Efvk.

Cohn, Nate, "Explaining Hillary Clinton's Lost Ground in the Polls." *The New York Times*, May 24, 2016. www.nytimes.com/2016/05/25/upshot/explaining-hillary-clintons-lost-ground-in-the-polls.html?smid=fb-share.

Cohn, Nate and Monkovic, Toni, "Bernie Sanders and rigged elections." *The New York Times*, June 1, 2016. www.nytimes.com/2016/06/02/upshot/bernie-sanders-and-rigged-elections-sometimes-you-just-lose.html?smid=fb-share.

Cohn, Jonathan, "Hillary Clinton Is A Progressive Democrat, Despite What You May Have Heard." *Huffington Post*, May 8, 2016. www.huffingtonpost.com/entry/hillary-clinton-progressive_us_572cca08e4b0b-c9cb0469098.

Coppinger, Mike, "Colin Kaepernick: 'Embarrassing' that Donald Trump, Hillary Clinton are candidates." *USA Today*, September 27, 2016. www.usatoday.com/story/sports/nfl/49ers/2016/09/27/colin-kaepernick-don-ald-trump-hillary-clinton-debate/91181232/.

CNN Politics, "Bernie Sanders pledges to defeat Donald Trump." CNN, June 17, 2016. www.cnn.com/videos/pol-itics/2016/06/17/bernie-sanders-pledges-to-defeat-don-ald-trump-vosot-cnni.cnn.

Evans, Sara, *Personal Politics*, N.Y.: Vintage, 1980.

Freedman, Estelle, *No Turning Back: The History of Feminism and the Future of Women*, N,Y.: Ballantine, 2002.

Frizell, Sam and Keene, N.H., "Sanders Suggests Clinton Is Not a True Progressive." *Time*, February 2, 2016. www.time.com/4205149/bernie-sanders-hillary-clinton-progres-sive/.

Garcia, Feliks, "Susan Sarandon: Hillary Clinton is 'more dangerous' than Donald Trump." *The Independent*, June 3, 2016. www.independent.co.uk/news/people/susan-sarandon-hillary-clinton-more-dangerous-don-ald-trump-a7064826.html.

Gauthier, Brendan, "Watch: Frustrated Bernie Sanders walks

out on hostile TV news interview." *Salon,* March 18, 2016. www.salon.com/2016/03/18/watch_frustrated_bernie_sanders_walks_out_on_hostile_tv_news_interview/.

Golshan, Tara, "Hillary Clinton's feminism: a conversation with Rebecca Traister." Vox, September 27, 2016. www.vox.com/2016/9/4/12710840/hillary-clinton-feminism-conversation-rebecca-traister.

Grant, Adam and Sandberg, Sheryl, "Speaking While Female: Sheryl Sandberg and Adam Grant on Why Women Stay Quiet at Work." *The New York Times,* January 12, 2015. www.nytimes.com/2015/01/11/opinion/sunday/speaking-while-female.html.

Hernandez, Greg, "Hillary Clinton issues second apology for her inaccurate comments about Nancy Reagan and AIDS, GregInHollywood, March 12, 2016. http://greginhollywood.com/hillary-clinton-issues-second-apology-for-her-innacurate-comments-about-nancy-regan-and-aids-127686

Kazin, Michael, "Who Is the Real Progressive: Hillary Clinton or Bernie Sanders?: Both/And." *The Nation,* February 24, 2016. Accessed January 23, 2017. www.thenation.com/article/who-is-the-real-progressive-hillary-clinton-or-bernie-sanders/.

Krugman, Paul, "The Pastrami Principle." *The New York Times,* April 15, 2016. www.nytimes.com/2016/04/15/opinion/the-pastrami-principle.html?smprod=nytcore-ipad&smid=nytcore-ipad-share.

Lawrence, Jennifer, "Jennifer Lawrence: 'Why Do I Make Less Than My Male CoStars?'." *Lenny,* October 14, 2015. www.lennyletter.com/work/a147/jennifer-lawrence-why-do-i-make-less-than-my-male-costars/.

Luxenburg, Wendy, "The real danger when Donald Trump and Bernie Sanders call the system 'rigged'." Daily News Bin, June 11, 2016. www.dailynewsbin.com/opinion/the-danger-trump-and-sanders-present-by-calling-the-system-rigged/24964/.

Marcotte, Amanda, "Progressivism doesn't die with Hillary Clinton." *Salon,* April 11, 2016.

Martin, Jonathan, "Young Blacks Voice Skepticism on Hillary Clinton, Worrying Democrats." *The New York Times,* September 4, 2016. www.nytimes.com/2016/09/05/us/politics /young-blacks-voice-skepticism-on-hillary-clinton-worrying-democrats.html.

McEwan, Melissa, "Losing Control: Bernie Says Hillary Is the 'Lesser of Two Evils'." Blue Nation Review, May 21, 2016. www.bluenationreview.com/losing-control-bernie-says-hillary-is-the-lesser-of-two-evils/.

Milbank, Dana, "The sexist double standards hurting Hillary Clinton." *The Washington Post,* February 12, 2016. www .washingtonpost.com/opinions/the-sexist-double-standards-hurting-hillary-clinton/2016/02/12/ fb551e38-d195-11e5-abc9-ea152f0b9561_story.html? postshare=8411455399760965&tid=ss_fb&utm_term= .35aff24b9590.

Morrison, Susan, *Thirty Ways of Looking at Hillary,* New York: Harper, 2008.

Page, Susan and Ung, Jenny, "Poll shows that Millennials would flock to Clinton against Trump." *USA Today,* March 14, 2016. www.usatoday.com/story/news/politics/elections/2016/03/14/poll-millennials-clinton-sanders-trump-president/81612520/.

Pollitt, Katha, "Why Bernie Didn't Get My Vote." *The Nation,* May 4, 2016. www.thenation.com/article/why-bernie-didnt-get-my-vote/.

Saraiya, Sonia, "Feel the Bern, indeed: Sanders takes the low road with nasty Clinton tweet, undermining the promise of his campaign." *Salon,* March 16, 2016. www.salon .com/2016/03/16/feel_the_bern_indeed_sanders_takes_ the_low_road_with_nasty_clinton_tweet_undermining_the_promise_of_his_campaign/.

Schultz, Connie, "Same Misogyny, Different Season." Creators, April 20, 2016. https://www.creators.com/read/connie-schultz/04/16/same-misogyny-different-season.

Shorto, Russell, "Bernie Sanders's Forty-Year-Old Idea." *The New Yorker,* April 17, 2016. www.newyorker.com/news /news-desk/bernie-sanderss-forty-year-old-idea.

Small, Jay Newton, "Hillary Clinton Speaks, Male Pundits Hear Shouting." *Time*, March 16, http://time.com/4260665 /hillary-clinton-shouting/.

Wilstein, Matt, "Susan Sarandon: Trump Might Be Better for America Than Hillary Clinton." *The Daily Beast*, March 29, 2016. www.thedailybeast.com/articles/2016/03/29/susan -sarandon-trump-might-be-better-for-america-than-hillary-clinton.html.

Zeleny, Jeff, "Bernie or bust: Sanders supporters vow to hold out." CNN, June 2, 2016. www.cnn.com/2016/06/01 /politics/bernie-sanders-hillary-clinton-bernie-or-bust/index.html.

Zeleny, Jeff, "Obama Clinches Nomination; First Black Candidate to Lead a Major Party Ticket." *The New York Times*, June 4, 2008. www.nytimes.com/2008/06/04/us/politics /04elect.html?mwrsm=Facebook.

4. "Untrustworthy Hillary"

Abramson, Jill, "This may shock you: Hillary Clinton is fundamentally honest." *The Guardian*, March 28, 2016. www.theguardian.com/commentisfree/2016/mar/28 /hillary-clinton-honest-transparency-jill-abramson.

Alcindor, Yamiche and Rappeport, Alan, "Bernie Sanders Announces Plan for Speech at Vatican and Clarifications Follow." *The New York Times*, April 8, 2016. https:// www.nytimes.com/politics/first-draft/2016/04/08 /bernie-sanders-announces-plan-for-speech-at-vatican/?smid=fb-share&_r=0.

Beau, H. D., "Donald Trump Won Because of Facebook." *Slashdot*, November 9, 2016. www.tech.slashdot.org/story/16 /11/09/224219/donald-trump-won-because-of-facebook.

Bedard, Paul, "3 of 4 NYT bestsellers are anti-Clinton books." *Washington Examiner*, August 2, 2016. www.washington-examiner.com/3-of-4-nyt-bestsellers-are-anti-clinton-books/article/2598379.

Bernstein, Adam, "Richard Jewell: Wrongly Linked to Olympic Bombing." *The Washington Post*, August 30, 2007. http://www.washingtonpost.com/wp-dyn/content/article/2007/08/29/AR2007082901624.html.

Blow, Charles M., "Donald Trump is lying in plain sight." *The New York Times*, September 8, 2016. www.nytimes.com/2016/09/08/opinion/donald-trump-is-lying-in-plain-sight.html?action=click&contentCollection=Politics&module=Trending&version=Full&region=Marginalia&pgtype=article.

Boorstin, Daniel, *The Image: A Guide to Pseudo-events in America*, N.Y.: Vintage, 1961.

Bordo, Susan, "5 Ways Broadcast News Is Ruining The 2016 Election." *Huffington Post*, August 29, 2016. www.huffingtonpost.com/susan-bordo-/5-ways-broadcast-news-is-ruining-the-election_b_11735996.html.

Bordo, Susan, "P.C., O.J., and Truth," *Twilight Zones*, Berkeley: University of California Press, 1999.

Bordo, Susan, "Hillary Clinton, The Media, And The "Optics" Of Untrustworthiness." *Huffington Post*, July 7, 2016. www.huffingtonpost.com/susan-bordo-/hillary-clinton-the-media_b_10834828.html.

Bordo, Susan, "What the Difference Between 'Re-Setting' and Lying?" *Huffington Post*, August 20, 2016. http://www.huffingtonpost.com/susan-bordo-/whats-the-difference-betw_12_b_11612674.html.

Bruni, Frank, "Hillary health shocker." *The New York Times*, August 23, 2016. www.nytimes.com/2016/08/24/opinion/hillary-health-shocker.html?smid=fb-share.

Bump, Philip, "How to be a 'straight shooter' like Donald Trump, in 7 easy steps." *The Washington Post*, July 20, 2015. https://www.washingtonpost.com/news/the-fix/wp/2015/07/20/how-to-be-a-straight-shooter-like-donald-trump-in-7-easy-steps/?utm_term=.78fcedf748da

Burleigh, Nina, "Hillary Clinton's Woman Problem Explained." *Newsweek*, September 5, 2015. www.newsweek.com/hillary-clinton-women-problem-explained-369153.

capkronos (*Daily Kos* member), "Harvard Study Confirms

Anti-ClintonMedia Bias." *Daily Kos,* June 26, 2016. www.dailykos.com/story/2016/6/26/1542758/-Harvard-Study-Confirms-Anti-Clinton-Media-Bias.

Chemaly, Soraya, "People Think Women Lie Because That's What We Teach Our Children." *Huffington Post,* September 11, 2014. www.huffingtonpost.com/soraya-chemaly/people-think-women-lie-because-thats-what-we-teach-children_b_5805532.html.

Cohn, Jonathan, "If The Media Treated Trump Like Other Candidates, Yesterday Would Have Ended His Campaign." *Huffington Post,* June 1, 2016. www.huffingtonpost.com/entry/donald-trump-media_us_574f07c1e4b0ed-593f12e5d0.

Collinson, Stephen, "Donald Trump attempts to reboot." CNN, August 9, 2016. www.cnn.com/2016/08/09/politics/donald-trump-republicans-paul-ryan/index.html.

Daou, Peter, "Hillary Clinton Is One of the Most Ethical (and Most Lied About) Political Leaders in America." *Blue Nation Review,* August 12, 2016. www.bluenationreview.com/hillary-clinton-is-one-of-the-most-ethical-and-most-lied-about-political-leaders-in-america/.

Daou, Peter, "Let It Go, Media: Hillary Clinton Does NOT Have a Trust and Honesty Problem." *Blue Nation Review,* July 25, 2016. www.bluenationreview.com/hillary-clinton-does-not-have-a-trust-and-honesty-problem/.

Daou, Peter, "MYTHBUSTED: How Millions of Hillary Voters Triumphed Over Insidious Media Narratives." *Blue Nation Review,* March 19, 2016. www.bluenationreview.com/millions-of-hillary-voters-triumphed-over-media-narratives/.

Daou, Peter, "Trust Me, Hillary Supporters: The Media Will NOT Be Your Friend In 2016." *Blue Nation Review,* May 27, 2016. wwwbluenationreview.com/hillary-supporters-the-media-will-not-be-your-friend-in-2016/.

Dewey, Caitlin, "The only true winners of this election are trolls." *The Washington Post,* November 3, 2016. www.washingtonpost.com/news/the-intersect/wp/2016/11/03/the-only-true-winners-of-this-election-are-trolls/?utm_term=.c21ac6a1d867.

DeYoung, Karen and Goldman, Adam, "Dems' Benghazi report: Clinton 'engaged' during attack, panels 'squandered millions of taxpayer dollars," *Chcago Tribune*, June 27, 2016. http://www.chicagotribune.com/news/ct-benghazi-report-democrats-20160627-story.html.

Dicker, Ron, "Stephen Colbert Has Finally Figured Out Hillary Clinton's Illness." *Huffington Post*, August 24, 2016. www.huffingtonpost.com/entry/stephen-colbert-has-finally-figured-out-hillary-clintons-illness_us_57bd6465e4b03d51368ba471?.

"Did Donald Trump's Trip to Mexico Pay Off," *Meet the Press, NBC News*, August 31, 2016.

Easley, Jason, "One Chart Exposes How The Media Bashes Hillary Clinton While Promoting Donald Trump." Politicus USA, June 18, 2016. www.politicususa.com/2016/06/18/chart-exposes-media-bashes-hillary-clinton-promoting-donald-trump.html.

Freeman, Hadley, "Imagine if Donald Trump were a woman. You simply can't." *The Guardian*, September 27, 2016. www.theguardian.com/commentisfree/2016/sep/27/donald-trump-woman-hillary-clinton-presidential-debate.

Gabbatt, Adam and Jamieson, Amber, "'You don't fit the image': Hillary Clinton's decades-long push against a sexist press." *The Guardian*, September 15, 2016. www.theguardian.com/us-news/2016/sep/15/hillary-clinton-press-sexism-media-interviews.

Garcia, Ahiza and Lear, Justin, "5 stunning fake news stories that reached millions." *CNN Money*, November 2, 2016. www.money.cnn.com/2016/11/02/media/fake-news-stories/.

Garossino, Sandy, "What's written in the scars of Hillary Clinton." *National Observer*, August 1, 2016. www.national-observer.com/2016/08/01/analysis/whats-written-scars-hillary-clinton.

Graves, Lucia, "Why Are People Calling Hillary Clinton and Carly Fiorina Liars?" *Glamour*, October 12, 2015. www

.glamour.com/story/why-are-people-calling-hillary.

Gallagher, Brenden, "The Most Sexist Things Donald Trump Has Said About Hillary Clinton (So Far)." VH1, September 27, 2016. www.vh1.com/news/283594/donald-trump-sexist-hillary-clinton-comments/.

Gabler, Neal, "Farewell, America." *Moyers and Company*, November 10, 2016. http://billmoyers.com/story/fare-well-america/.

Gunter, Jen, "I'm a doctor these are the things I find concerning with Trump's medical letter." *Dr. Jen Gunter*, August 16, 2016. www.drjengunter.wordpress.com/2016/08/16/im-a-doctor-these-are-the-things-i-find-concerning-with-trumps-medical-letter/.

Hananoki, Eric, "It's Not Just Trump Fans; His Media Supporters Also Call Clinton A 'Bitch'." *Media Matters*, June 16, 2016. www.mediamatters.org/blog/2016/06/16/it-s-not-just-trump-fans-his-media-supporters-also-call-clinton-bitch/210998.

Harvey, Chelsea, "Here's how scientific misinformation, such as climate doubt, spreads through social media." *The Washington Post*, January 4, 2016. www.washing-tonpost.com/news/energy-environment/wp/2016/01/04/heres-how-scientific-misinformation-such-as-cli-mate-doubt-spreads-through-social-media/?utm_term=.f28f4a913dd7.

"He couldn't even get this right: Trump's trip," *Morning Joe*, MSNBC, September 1, 2016. http://www.msnbc.com/morning-joe/watch/he-couldn-t-even-get-this-right-trump-s-trip-755766339528.

Hightower, Jim, "Donnie's little lies are yuuuge: Trump has redefined what it means to be deceitful on the campaign trail." *Salon*, August 18, 2016. www.salon.com/2016/08/18/donnies-little-lies-are-yuuuge-trump-has-redefined-what-it-means-to-be-deceitful-on-the-campaign-trail/.

Holyk, Gegory and Langer, Gary, "Poll: Clinton Unpopularity at New High, on Par With Trump." ABC News, August 31, 2016. www.abcnews.go.com/Politics/poll-

clinton-unpopularity-high-par-trump/story
?id=41752050&cid=share_facebook_widget.

Isaac, Mike, "Facebook, in Cross Hairs After Election, Is
Said to Question Its Influence." *New York Times*, November 12, 2016. www.nytimes.com/2016/11/14/technology
/facebook-is-said-to-question-its-influence-in-election
.html.

Israel, Josh and Raymond, Laurel, "The Origin Of The Trump
Campaign's Bizarre Obsession With Hillary Clinton's
Brain." *ThinkProgress*, August 19, 2016. www.thinkprog-
ress.org/trump-campaigns-bizarre-hillary-health-ob-
session-e781284405c0#.zd923cchr.

Jacobson, Louis, "Yes, Donald Trump did call climate change
a hoax." Politifact, June 3, 2016, http://www.politifact
.com/truth-o-meter/statements/2016/jun/03/hillary-
clinton/yes-donald-trump-did-call-climate-change-chi-
nese-h/Trump.

kmassa, "Hillary Clinton and the Battle Against Ghosts of Misogyny Past." Medium, May 10, 2016. www.medium.com
/@kmassa/hillary-clinton-and-the-battle-against-
ghosts-of-misogyny-past-780cc18c30ec.

Krugman, Paul, "Both Sides Now?" *The New York Times*, July 18,
2016. www.nytimes.com/2016/07/18/opinion/both-sides
-now.html?campaign_id=A100&campaign_type=E-
mail&_r=0.

Kuhn, Thomas, *The Structure of Scientific Revolutions*, Chicago: University of Chicago Press, 1970.

Kuntzman, Gersh, "Clinton's cover story for her pneumonia
diagnosis further proves her first instinct is to lie," New
York *Daily News*, September 12, 2016. http://www.ny-
dailynews.com/news/politics/clinton-pneumonia-cov-
er-story-proves-instinct-lie-article-1.2788402.

LaCapria, Kim, "Snopes' Field Guide to Fake News Sites and
Hoax Purveyors." Snopes.com, January 6, 2017. www
.snopes.com/2016/01/14/fake-news-sites/.

Lee, Bruce Y., "Health Misinformation Abounds On Pinterest, Instagram And Visual Social Media." *Forbes*, January 27, 2016. www.forbes.com/sites/brucelee/2016/01/27

/health-misinformation-on-pinterest-instagram-and-vi-sual-social-media/.

Lewis, Bobby, "The Six Worst Media Reactions to Hillary Clinton's Pneumonia Diagnosis." Media Matters for America, September 12, 2016. https://mediamatters.org/research/2016/09/12/six-worst-media-reactions-hillary-clintons-pneumonia-diagnosis/213012

Mandelbaum, Ryan F., "Is digital photography real? Searching for truth in digital photojournalism." *Science Line*, October 3, 2016. www.scienceline.org/2016/10/is-digital-photography-real/.

"Bad sushi." YouTube, video July 23, 2006. www.youtube.com/watch?v=XnOnDatqENo&feature=youtu.be.

Marten, Donn, "*Washington Post* Outraged That Some Call Hillary a Bitch." *Downtrend*, June 17, 2016. www.downtrend.com/donn-marten/washington-post-outraged-that-some-call-hillary-a-bitch.

McEwan, Melissa, "MYTHBUSTER: Former NYT Editor Says Hillary Is Fundamentally Honest and Trustworthy." *Blue Nation Review*, March 28, 2016. www.bluenationreview.com/former-nyt-editor-says-hillary-is-fundamentally-honest-and-trustworthy/.

Media Matters Staff, "On MSNBC's *All In*, Media Matters' Eric Boehlert Details The Problematic Consequences Of Washington Post's Erroneous Clinton Email Report." Media Matters for America, March 31, 2016. www.mediamatters.org/video/2016/03/31/on-msnbcs-all-in-media-matters-eric-boehlert-de/209674.

Millhiser, Ian, "The dark history of how false balance journalism enabled lynching." *ThinkProgress*, December 14, 2016. Accessed January 23, 2017. https://thinkprogress.org/the-dark-history-of-how-false-balance-journalism-enabled-lynching-284f2291b4a1.

Mirkinson, Jack, "*Morning Joe*'s pathetic Trump temper tantrum: Joe & Mika pretend to be objective—and fail miserably." *Salon*, February 19, 2016. www.salon.com/2016/02/19/morning_joes_pathetic_trump_temper_tantrum_joe_mika_pretend_to_be_objective_ and_fail_miserably/.

Morning Joe, "Filmmaker Reiner has serious words for Trump." MSNBC, May 5, 2016. www.msnbc.com/morning-joe/watch/filmmaker-reiner-has-serious-words-for-trump-679858243664.

Morning Joe, "*Morning Joe* Panel: Trump Throws Out Red Meat," MSNBC, September 2, 2016.

MSNBC Live with Stephanie Ruhlie, "Trump Campaign: No plans to review lab results with Dr. Oz." MSNBC, September 14, 2016. www.msnbc.com/stephanie-ruhle/watch/no-plans-to-review-lab-results-with-dr-oz-764746819709.

The New York Times Editorial Board, "Cutting Ties to the Clinton Foundation." *The New York Times*, August 30, 2016. www.nytimes.com/2016/08/30/opinion/cutting-ties-to-the-clinton-foundation.html?smid=fb-share.

"An Open Letter Regarding Climate Change from Concerned Members of the U.S. National Academy of Sciences." Responsible Scientists.Org, September 20, 2016. http://responsiblescientists.org.

Oremus, Will, "Mark Zuckerberg Says Fake News on Facebook Had 'No Impact' on the Election." *Slate*, November 10, 2016. www.slate.com/blogs/future_tense/2016/11/10/mark_zuckerberg_says_fake_news_on_facebook_had_no_impact_on_election.html.

Palmer, Bill, "2016 election is teaching us that career politicians are more honest than their biggest detractors." Daily News Bin, July 4, 2016. www.dailynewsbin.com/opinion/2016-election-is-teaching-us-that-career-politicians-arent-nearly-as-bad-as-their-biggest-detractors/25079/.

Palmer, Bill, "Chris Christie uses speech to 'convict' Hillary Clinton before he heads to prison for BridgeGate." Daily News Bin, July 19, 2016. www.dailynewsbin.com/opinion/chris-christie-inexplicably-sides-with-gaddafi-and-terrorists-while-attacking-hillary-clinton/25285/.

Palmer, Bill, "Fact checkers confirm Hillary Clinton is more honest than any of her 2016 opponents." Daily News Bin,

March 20, 2016. www.dailynewsbin.com/news/fact-checkers-confirm-hillary-clinton-is-more-honest-than-any-of-her-2016-opponents/24196/.

Parton, Heather Digby, "Press, lies and Hillary's campaign: Years of smears have created a fictional version of Clinton. They're also a disservice to voters." *Salon*, September 6, 2016. www.salon.com/2016/09/06/press-lies-and-hillarys-campaign-years-of-smears-have-created-a-fictional-version-of-clinton-theyre-also-a-disservice-to-voters/.

Pooley, Jefferson, "Why We Can't Know Whether Facebook Is to Blame for Trump's Election." *Slate*, November 11, 2016. www.slate.com/blogs/future_tense/2016/11/11/we_can_t_know_whether_facebook_is_to_blame_for_trump_s_win.html.

Poundstone, William, "The Internet Isn't Making Us Dumber —It's Making Us More 'Meta-Ignorant'." *New York Maazine*, July 27, 2016. www.nymag.com/scienceofus/2016/07/the-internet-isnt-making-us-dumber-its-making-us-more-meta-ignorant.html.

Raymond, Laurel, "The Origin of the Trump Campaign's Bizarre Obsession with Hillary Clinton's Brain." ThinkProgress, August 19, 2016. https://thinkprogress.org/trump-campaigns-bizarre-hillary-health-obsession-e781284405c0#.e1tkrmvj2.

Read, Max, "Can Facebook Solve Its Macedonian Fake-News Problem?" *New York Magazine*, November 4, 2016. www.nymag.com/selectall/2016/11/can-facebook-solve-its-macedonian-fake-news-problem.html.

Rogers, Buck, "Exposed Viral Hoaxes Prove How Easy It Is To Dupe The World With Disinfo." *Activist Post*, October 22, 2016. www.activistpost.com/2016/10/exposed-viral-hoaxes-prove-easy-dupe-world-disinfo.html.

Rubin, Jennifer, "Hillary skewers Trump on racism." *The Washington Post*, August 25, 2016. https://www.washingtonpost.com/blogs/right-turn/wp/2016/08/25/hillary-skewers-trump-on-racism/?utm_term=.b9ae1ec0dfd0.

Schauffler, Marina, "In post-fact society, emotions and

ideology increasingly squelch scientific evidence." *Press Herald*, October 30, 2016. www.pressherald.com /2016/10/30/sea-change-in-post-fact-society-emotions-and-ideology-increasingly-squelch-scientific-evidence/.

Stark, Steven, *Glued to the Set*, N.Y.: Simon and Schuster, 1997.

Valenti, Jessica, "Hillary Clinton's problem? We just don't trust women." *The Guardian*, September 22, 2016. www .theguardian.com/commentisfree/2016/sep/22/hillary-clinton-women-trust.

Waldman, Paul, "Here's a tale of two scandals: Guess which one will get more play?." *The Washington Post*, September 2, 2016. www.washingtonpost.com/blogs/plumline/wp/2016/09/02/heres-a-tale-of-two-scandals-guess-which-one-will-get-more-play/?utm_term =.592529a556af.

Walsh, Joan, "A Lot of Trump Supporters are Deplorable—and a Lot of the Media Are Too." *The Nation*, September 12, 2016.

The Washington Post Editorial Board, "Trump lies and lies and lies again." *The Washington Post*, May 25, 2016. www.washingtonpost.com/opinions/counting-donald-trumps-lies/2016/05/25/bc0d93a8-229f-11e6-aa84-42391ba52c91_story.html?postshare= 9541464344731884&tid=ss_fb-bottom&utm_term=. bae1fd12c6a0.

Wemple, Erik, "Study: Clinton-Trump coverage was a feast of false equivalency." *The Washington Post*, December 7, 2016. https://www.washingtonpost.com/blogs/erik-wemple/wp/2016/12/07/study-clinton-trump-coverage-was-a-feast-of-false-equivalency/?utm_term =.2d95db3411c6.

Wemple, Erik, "False equivalence: Chuck Todd says Clinton will follow Trump to 'low road'." *The Washington Post*, May 4, 2016. https://www.washingtonpost.com/blogs /erik-wemple/wp/2016/05/04/false-equivalence-chuck-todd-says-clinton-will-follow-trump-to-low-road/?tid=a_inl&utm_term=.b47588666c72.

Williams,MaryElizabeth,"Hillarypowersthroughpneumonia —becausethat'swhatwomendo." *Salon*,September12,2016. www.salon.com/2016/09/12/hillary-powers-through-pneumonia-because-thats-what-women-do/?source =newsletter.

Wilson, Jeremy, "How fake viral photos manipulate your emotions." *Kernel Magazine*, January 21, 2013. www .kernelmag.dailydot.com/features/report/8531/ how-fake-viral-photos-manipulate-your-emotions/.

Yglesias, Matthew, "Colin Powell's foundation and Hillary Clinton's are treated very differently by the media." Vox, August 30, 2016. www.vox.com/policy-and-politics/2016/8/30/12690444/alma-powell-clinton-foundation.

Zanotti, Emily, "Bernie Bros Harassing Hillary Clinton's Women Supporters—Rise of the Alt-Left." *HeatStreet*, May 31, 2016. www.heatst.com/politics/bernie-bros-out-for-hillary-clintons-blood-online-rise-of-the-alt-left/.

5. Damned Emails

"A Comprehensive Guide to Benghazi Myths and Facts," MmfA, http://mediamatters.org.

BNR Team, "DEVELOPING: New State Dept. Revelation of Classified Marking Error Supports Hillary on Emails." *Blue Nation Review*, July 6, 2016. www.bluenationreview.com/revelation-of-classified-marking-error-supports-hillary-on-emails/.

Bordo, Susan and Palmer, Thomas, "Enough About The Damned Emails!" *Huffington Post*, August 11, 2016. www.huffingtonpost.com/susan-bordo-/enough-about-the-damned-emails_b_11403456.html.

Bordo, Susan, "What's the Difference Between "Re-setting" and Lying? According to *Morning Joe*: Trump Does One and Hillary Does the Other." *Bordo Crossings*, August 19, 2016. www.bordocrossings.com/single-post/2016/08/19

/What%E2%80%99s-the-Difference-Between-%E2%80%9CRe-setting%E2%80%9D-and-Lying-According-to-Morning-Joe-Trump-Does-One-and-Hillary-Does-the-Other.

Bordo, Susan, "Who Really Lied About Clinton's Emails?" Bordo Crossings, September 22, 2016. www.bordocrossings.com/single-post/2016/09/22/Who-Really-Lied-About-Clintons-Emails.

Bradner, Eric and Zeleny, Jeff, "Clinton's email excuse won't quiet critics," *CNN Politics,* March 17, 2015. http://www.cnn.com/2015/03/10/politics/hillary-clinton-email-press-conference-analysis/Ev.

Committee on Oversight and Reform, "State IG Confirms Longstanding and Widespread Personal Email Use by Secretaries of State and their Staff." *Committee on Oversight and Reform,* May 25, 2016. www.democrats-oversight.house.gov/news/press-releases/state-ig-confirms-longstanding-and-widespread-personal-email-use-by-secretaries.

Cummings, Elijah E., "Cummings Releases Full Powell Email Advising Clinton on Personal Email Use." *Medium,* September 7, 2016. www.medium.com/oversightdems/cummings-releases-full-powell-email-advising-clinton-on-personal-email-use-65904c1ccfa#.pbe7dlf9d.

DeYoung, Karen and Goldman, Adam, "Dems' Benghazi report: Clinton 'engaged' during attack, panel 'squandered millions of taxpayer dollars'." *Chicago Tribune,* June 27, 2016. www.chicagotribune.com/news/ct-benghazi-report-democrats-20160627-story.html.

Dovere, Edward-Isaac, "Inside the Loss Clinton Saw Coming." Politico, November 9, 2016. www.politico.com/magazine/story/2016/11/hillary-clinton-loses-2016-election-214439.

Edwards, Julia, "Here's Why Hillary Clinton Email Scandal Didn't Rise To Level Of 'Gross Negligence'." *Huffington Post,* July 6, 2016. www.huffingtonpost.com/entry/hillary-clinton-email-scandal_us_577d08f8e4b09b4c43c1a785.

Eichenwald, Kurt, "How *'The New York Times'* Bungled the

Hillary Clinton Emails Story." *Newsweek*, July 24, 2015. www.newsweek.com/hillary-clinton-new-york-times-emails-357246.

Eichenwald, Kurt, "Why Hillary Clinton's 'Emailgate' Is a Fake Scandal." *Newsweek*, March 10, 2015. www.newsweek .com/hillary-clinton-emailgate-312784.

"FBI Dir: Our view is no charges in this case," *MSNBC Live*, July 5, 2016. http://www.msnbc.com/msnbc-news/watch/fbi-dir-on-clinton-email-investigation-718710851539.

Fields, Jeffrey, "Here's How Classified Information Got Into Those Hillary Clinton Emails?" *Huffington Post*, July 19, 2016. www.huffingtonpost.com/the-conversation-us /how-did-classified-inform_b_11074304.html.

Griswold, Alex, "Poll: Majority Disagree with FBI Decision Not to Charge Hillary Clinton," *Mediaite*, July 11, 2016. http://www.mediaite.com/election-2016/poll-majority-disagree-with-fbi-decision-not-to-charge-hillary-clinton/.

Hartmann, Margaret, "Why the Clinton Campaign Is Feuding With the New York *Times*." *New York Magazine*, July 31, 2015. www.nymag.com/daily/intelligencer/2015/07 /hillary-clinton-new-york-times.html.

Hains, Tim, "Full Interview: Hillary Clinton on *Fox News Sunday*," RCP, July 31, 2016. http://www.realclearpolitics.com/video/2016/07/31/full_interview_hillary_clinton_on_fox_news_sunday.html.

"Joe: I question James Comey's courage," *Morning Joe*, MSNBC, July 6, 2016. http://www.msnbc.com/morning-joe/watch/joe-i-question-james-comey-s-courage-719352387765.

King, John, "Clinton's email scandal is exactly what you can expect from her presidential campaign." CNN, March 11, 2015. www.cnn.com/2015/03/10/politics/hillary-clinton-emails-flashback/.

McAuliff, Michael, "Hillary Clinton's Multiple Servers And Phones Weren't So Multiple." *Huffington Post*, July 6, 2016. www.huffingtonpost.com/entry/hillary-clinton-james-comey-email-servers_us_577d35cbe4b0a629c1ab7bdb.

O'Donnell, Jayne, "Justice Dept.: Clinton allowed to delete personal emails." *USA Today*, September 12, 2015. www .usatoday.com/story/news/2015/09/12/justice-dept-clinton-emails/72144988/.

Palmer, Bill, "CNN and MSNBC confirm Hillary Clinton will not face any charges in email inquiry." Daily News Bin, July 2, 2016. www.dailynewsbin.com/news/msnbc-confirms-hillary-clinton-will-face-any-charges-in-email-inquiry/25073/.

Palmer, Bill, "FBI reveals Colin Powell told Hillary Clinton to use private email at State Department." Daily News Bin, August 19, 2016. www.dailynewsbin.com/news/fbi-reveals-colin-powell-told-hillary-clinton-to-use-private-email/25747/.

Palmer, Thom, "Field guide to defending Hillary Clinton against every lie still being told about her email." Daily News Bin, July 8, 2016. www.dailynewsbin.com/news/field-guide-to-defending-hillary-clinton-against-the-non-concluded-phony-email-scandal/25114/.

Purdum, Todd S., "What's Really Ailing Hillary." Politico Magazine, September 16, 2016. www.politico.com/magazine/story/2016/09/hillary-clinton-media-transparency-214250.

The Rachel Maddow Show, "Clinton e-mail report illustrates antiquated IT system." MSNBC, May 25, 2016. www.msnbc .com/rachel-maddow/watch/clinton-e-mail-report-shows-broken-it-system-693093443953.

"Representative Elijah Cummings Questions FBI Director James Comey," YouTube video, July 7, 2016. https://www .youtube.com/watch?v=syU0WZovTFg.

"Representative Matt Cartwright questions FBI director James Comey about Classified Headers." YouTube video, July 7, 2016. https://www.youtube.com /watch?v=Fn-p-Cpskiw&app=desktop.

Shear, Michael D., "Attorney General accepts recommendation not to charge Hillary Clinton." *The New York Times,* July 6, 2016. www.nytimes.com/2016/07/07/us/politics /hillary-clinton-loretta-lynch.html?smid=fb-share.

Tiefer, Charles, "State Department Report On Email Vindicates Clinton Rather Than Nails Her." *Forbes*, May 25, 2016. www.forbes.com/sites/charlestiefer/2016/05/25/state-department-report-on-email-vindicates-clinton-rather-than-nails-her/#3f1d74f92c7d.

The *Washington Post* Editorial Board, "The Hillary Clinton email story is out of control." *The Washington Post*, September 8, 2016. www.washingtonpost.com/opinions /the-hillary-clinton-email-story-is-out-of-control/ 2016/09/08/692947d0-75fc-11e6-8149-b8d05321db62 _story.html?utm_term=.88e9c966b516.

The *Washington Post* Editorial Board, "Hillary Clinton just made a very important announcement." *The Washington Post*, August 31, 2016. www.washingtonpost.com/opinions /clinton-just-made-a-very-important-announce-ment—and-hardly-anyone-is-talking-about-it/2016 /08/31/5379ddfe-6ef5-11e6-9705-23e51a2f424d_story .html?utm_term=.b26fe5a9dc75.

Yglesias, Matthew, "The real Clinton email scandal is that a bullshit story has dominated the campaign." Vox, November 4, 2016. http://www.vox.com/policy-and-politics/2016/11/4/13500018/clinton-email-scandal-bullshit.

6. A Tale of Two Conventions and One Hot Mic

20/20, "*20/20* Monica Lewinsky Interview March 3, 1999." YouTube video, May 23, 2016. https://www.youtube. com/watch?v=5mM0uCjqbfg.

Appelbaum, Yoni, "Michelle Obama's Speech for the Ages." *The Atlantic*, July 25, 2016. www.theatlantic.com/politics/ archive/2016/07/a-speech-for-the-ages/493010/?utm_ source=atlfb.

Bassett, Laura, "Women Won't Elect A Fat-Shamer-In-Chief." *Huffington Post*, September 29, 2016. www .huffingtonpost.com/entry/donald-trump-fat-shamer_us _57ed1dd6e4b024a52d2d15f9?ncid=engmodushpmg00000003.

Bedard, Paul, "3 of 4 NYT bestsellers are anti-Clinton books." *Washington Examiner*, August 2, 2016. www.washingtonexaminer.com/3-of-4-nyt-bestsellers-are-anti-clinton-books/article/2598379.

Blake, Aaron, "The first Trump-Clinton presidential debate transcript, annotated." *The Washington Post*, September 26, 2016. www.washingtonpost.com/news/the-fix/wp/2016/09/26/the-first-trump-clinton-presidential-debate-transcript-annotated/?utm_term=.d0b1d531330d.

The Briefing, "Trump victim: Alicia Machado: The Briefing." YouTube video, September 26, 2016. www.youtube.com/watch?v=U8ZM58O_gBo&feature=player_embedded.

Bordo, Susan, "Donald Trump's Fat-Phobia is a Global Issue." Daily News Bin, October 3, 2016. www.dailynewsbin.com/opinion/donald-trump-fat-phobia-global-issue/26171/.

Burns, Alexander and Corasaniti, Nick, "After a Disappointing Debate, Donald Trump goes on the attack." *The New York Times*, September 27, 2016. www.nytimes.com/2016/09/28/us/politics/hillary-clinton-donald-trump-debate.html?_r=0.

Carmon, Irin, "Poll: After Debate, Women Think Less of Trump and Better of Clinton," NBC News, September 29,2016. http://www.nbcnews.com/politics/2016-election/poll-after-debate-women-think-less-trump-better-clinton-n656321.

Cassidy, John, "Hillary Clinton's Plan to Squeeze the Ultra-Rich." *The New Yorker*, October 25, 2016. www.newyorker.com/news/john-cassidy/hillary-clintons-plan-to-squeeze-the-ultra-rich.

Christina, Greta, "Subtle sexism: 7 of the less-noted but still very problematic attacks on Hillary Clinton." *Salon*, August 25, 2016. www.salon.com/2016/08/25/subtle-sexism-7-of-the-less-noted-but-still-very-problematic-attacks-on-hillary-clinton_partner/.

Conason, Joe, "Former Whitewater Counsel Endorses Clinton—And Dismisses 'Scandals'." *The National Memo*,

October 7, 2016. www.nationalmemo.com/former-white-water-counsel-endorses-clinton-and-dismisses-scandals/.

Daou, Peter, "I've worked for both Clintons and Trump is playing with fire assailing their marriage." *Shareblue*, September 29, 2016. http://shareblue.com/ive-worked-for-both-clintons-and-trump-is-playing-with-fire-assailing-their-marriage/.

"Fact checks of the second presidential debate." *The New York Times*, October 9, 2016. www.nytimes.com/interactive/2016/10/09/us/elections/fact-check-debate.html?smid=fb-share.

FiveThirtyEight, "An 80 Percent Shot Doesn't Mean Clinton Is A Sure Thing." *FivethirtyEight*, June 30, 2016. www.fivethirtyeight.com/features/an-80-percent-shot-doesnt-mean-clinton-is-a-sure-thing/.

Freedman, Mia, "Dear Trump: I remember when a man 'grabbed me by the pussy'. I was 13. It's called sexual assault." *Mamamia*, October 8, 2016. www.mamamia.com.au/donald-trump-sexual-assault/.

Gray, Emma, "Donald Trump Couldn't Stop Interrupting Hillary Clinton On Debate Night." *Huffington Post*, September 26, 2016. www.huffingtonpost.com/entry/donald-trump-couldnt-stop-interrupting-hillary-clinton-on-debate-night_us_57e9ca11e4b024a52d2a0e26?ncid=fcbklnkushpmg00000063.

Hardball with Chris Matthews, "Let Me Finish: Hillary Clinton makes history." MSNBC, June 8, 2016. Accessed January 23, 2017. www.msnbc.com/hardball/watch/let-me-finish-hillary-clinton-makes-history-701791299925.

Healy, Patrick and Martin, Jonathan, "Democrats make Hillary Clinton a historic nominee." *The New York Times*, July 26, 2016. www.nytimes.com/2016/07/27/us/politics/dnc-speakers-sanders-clinton.html?action=click&contentCollection=Politics&module=RelatedCoverage&region=EndOfArticle&pgtype=article.

Healy, Patrick and Rappeport, Alan, "Trump is met with firestorm after lewd talk about women." *The Boston*

Globe, October 08, 2016. www.bostonglobe.com/news/ nation/2016/10/07/trump-recorded-having-extreme- ly-lewd-conversation-about-women/9oO4QD09XeXPx- vk4Y0AejI/story.html?event=event25.

Heffernan, Virginia, "Hillary and Monica." *Be Yourself*, May 2,2016.www.byrslf.co/hillary-and-monica-9b2a717747c9 #.wg49st15a.

Hoilman, Carly, "Why MSNBC's Rachel Maddow Found Start of Bill Clinton's DNC Speech 'Shocking and Weird'." TheBlaze, July 27, 2016. www.theblaze.com/news /2016/07/27/why-msnbcs-rachel-maddow-found-start- of-bill-clintons-dnc-speech-shocking-and-weird/.

Jones, Sarah, "Here Is Juanita Broaddrick's Affidavit That Destroys Trump's Attack On Hillary Clinton." Politicus USA, October 9, 2016. www.politicususa.com/2016/10/09/ sworn-affidavit-juanita-broaddrick-denies-allegations .html.

Krieg, Gregory, "Hillary Clinton hate on sale in the Streets of Cleveland," *CNN Politics*, July 21 2016. http://www.cnn. com/2016/07/21/politics/hillary-clinton-merchandise -cleveland-republican-convention/.

Lavender, Paige, "Hillary Clinton Responds To Donald Trump's 'Unhinged' Tweets With Her Own Fire Tweetstorm." *Huffington Post*, October 3, 2016. www.huffingtonpost .com/entry/hillary-clinton-donald-trump-women_ us_57ee7fe5e4b024a52d2e8322.

Legum, Gary, "The math is with Hillary: She's surging in the polls—and many Republicans are in denial." *Salon*, June 30, 2016. www.salon.com/2016/06/30/the_math_is_ with_hillary_she_surging_in_the_polls_and_many_re- publicans_are_in_denial/.

Marcotte, Amanda, "Anti-Clinton misogynists: If Bill's at- tackers are "defenders of women," why do they have a history of sexism?" *Salon*, January 12, 2016. Accessed January 23, 2017. www.salon.com/2016/01/12/anti_clin- ton_misogynists_if_bills_attackers_are_defenders_of_ women_why_do_they_have_a_history_of_sexism/.

Morrisson, Toni, "Comment." *The New Yorker*, October 5, 1998.

www.newyorker.com/magazine/1998/10/05/comment
-6543.

Palmer, Bill, "Donald Trump is already trying to weasel out of
debating Hillary Clinton." Daily News Bin, July 30, 2016.
www.dailynewsbin.com/opinion/donald-trump-lays-
the-groundwork-for-weaseling-out-of-debating-hillary-
clinton/25457/?utm_source=Daily+News+Bin&utm_
campaign=26591688eb-dailynewsbin_RSS_EMAIL
&utm_medium=email&utm_term=0_8a3553daba
-26591688eb-454631709.

Palmer, Bill, "First Lady Michelle Obama just gave the most important speech of the 2016 election." Daily News Bin, October 13, 2016. www.dailynewsbin.com/opinion/michelle
-obama-speech-2016/26300/.

Palmer, Bill, "Kenneth Starr, who once prosecuted Bill Clinton, just got fired over a sex scandal." Daily News Bin,
May 24, 2016. www.dailynewsbin.com/news/kenneth-
starr-who-once-prosecuted-bill-clinton-was-fired-to-
day-over-a-sex-scandal/24880/.

Palmer, Bill, "The real reason Trump is attacking Hillary over
Bill's past indiscretions (and why it won't work)." Daily News
Bin, May 9, 2016. http://www.dailynewsbin.com/opin-
ion/the-real-reason-trump-is-attacking-hillary-over-
bills-past-indiscretions-and-why-it-wont-work/24752/.

Palmer, Bill, "Republicans lose their minds after Bill Clinton
has harmless airport chat with AG Loretta Lynch." Daily
News Bin, June 30, 2016. www.dailynewsbin.com/opin-
ion/republicans-go-apeshit-after-bill-clinton-has-non-
event-meeting-with-ag-loretta-lynch/25062/.

Rodriguez, Germania, "Three New Polls Show Clinton Leading Trump." The National Memo, July 8, 2016. http://www
.nationalmemo.com/three-new-polls-show-clin-
ton-leading-trump/?utm_campaign=website&utm_
source=sd&utm_medium=email.

Silver, Nate, "Election Update: Where The Race Stands With
Three Weeks To Go." FiveThirtyEight, October 16, 2016.
www.fivethirtyeight.com/features/election-update-
where-the-race-stands-with-three-weeks-to-go/?ex_cid

=story-facebook.

Starr Commission, *The Starr Report*, Prima Lifestyles, September, 1998.

Terkel, Amanda, "America Has Finally Put A Woman At The Top Of The Ticket." *Huffington Post*, October 26, 2016. www .huffingtonpost.com/entry/hillary-clinton-nomination_ us_579a5228e4b0e2e15eb4f347.

Timm, Jane C., "Trump on Hot Mic: 'When You're a Star . . . You Can Do Anything' to Women." NBC News, October 7, 2016. www.nbcnews.com/politics/2016-election/trump-hot-mic-when-you-re-star-you-can-do-n662116.

Traister, Rebecca, "Bill Clinton Pulls Off a Presidential First: A First Lady Speech Delivered by a Man." *New York Magazine*, July 27, 2016. www.nymag.com/thecut/2016/07 /clinton-is-first-man-to-give-first-lady-speech.html.

Traister, Rebecca, "Michelle Obama Elegantly Eviscerated Donald Trump, Without Even Mentioning His Name." *New York Magazine*, July 26, 2016. www.nymag.com/daily /intelligencer/2016/07/michelle-obama-elegantly-eviscerated-trump.html?mid=fb-share-di.

"Trump Victim: Alicia Machado: The Briefing," September 26, 2016. https://www.youtube.com/watch?v=U8ZM58O_g Bo&feature=player_embedded.

Wright, David, "Poll: Clinton leads in four swing states." CNN, July 15, 2016. www.cnn.com/2016/07/15/politics/swing-state-polls-hillary-clinton-leads-trump/index.html.

7. Coup D'État

Allen, Jonathan, "Confessions of a Clinton reporter: The media's 5 unspoken rules for covering Hillary." *Vox*, July 6, 2015. www.vox.com/2015/7/6/8900143/hillary-clinton-reporting-rules.

America's Newsroom, "'*Clinton Cash*' Author: FBI Is Not 'Going Rogue' Based Just on My Book." *Fox News*, November 3, 2016. www.insider.foxnews.com/2016/11/03

/clinton-cash-author-fbi-not-going-rogue-based-just-my-book.

Bennett, Brian, "U.S. intelligence report says Putin targeted presidential election to 'harm' Hillary Clinton's chances." *Los Angeles Times*, January 6, 2017. www.latimes.com /nation/la-na-trump-russia-20170106-story.html.

Blow, Charles M., "Trump is an existential threat." *The New York Times*, November 3, 2016. www.nytimes.com /2016/11/03/opinion/campaign-stops/trump-is-an-existential-threat.html?smid=fb-share.

Bordo, Susan, "James Comey's Sins of Omission." *Huffington Post*, October 31, 2016. www.huffingtonpost.com /susan-bordo-/james-comeys-sins-of-omis_b_12735220 .html.

Burleigh, Nina, "THE PRESIDENTIAL ELECTION WAS A REFERENDUM ON GENDER AND WOMEN LOST." *Newsweek*, November 14, 2016. www.newsweek.com /2016/11/18/hillary-clinton-presidential-election-voter-gender-gap-520579.html.

"Sources reveal new details about reopened Hillary Clinton email investigation." CBS News, October 29, 2016. www.cbsnews.com/news/sources-reveal-new-details-reopened-hillary-clinton-email-investigation/?ftag=CNM-00-10aac3a.

Cillizza, Chris, "It's hard to see how James Comey could have handled this last 9 days any worse." *The Washington Post*, November 6, 2016. www.washingtonpost .com/news/the-fix/wp/2016/11/06/james-comey-totally-botched-the-last-10-days-of-the-2016-election/?utm _term=.2fc1c5440358.

Cohen, Richard, "Clinton survives another Salem trial." The *Washington Post*, July 11, 2016. www .washingtonpost.com/opinions/clinton-survives-another-salem-trial/2016/07/11/62435c92-478c-11e6-acbc-4d4870a079da_story.html.

Cole, David, *"What James Comey Did." The New York Review*, December 8, 2016. http://www.nybooks.com/articles /2016/12/08/what-james-comey-did/.

"Comey blinks! Hillary case closed." *World Net Daily*, November 6, 2016. www.wnd.com/2016/11/comey-blinks-hillary-case-closed/.

Dionne, E.J. Jr., "The costs of Comey's appeasement." *The Washington Post*, October 30, 2016. https://www.washingtonpost.com/opinions/comey-gives-in-to-shameful-partisanship/2016/10/30/c31c714a-9ed8-11e6-8d63-3e0a660f1f04_story.html?tid=hybrid_collaborative_1_na&utm_term=.8b8f63c83901.

Easley, Jason, "Bernie Sanders' Response Shows Why Nobody Cares About the Clinton Wikileaks Emails," Politicus USA, October 24, 2016. http://www.politicususa.com/2016/10/24/bernie-sanders-response-shows-cares-clinton-wikileaks-emails.html.

Fahrenthold, David A., "Trump's foundation ordered to stop fundraising." *Washington Post*, October 3, 2016. www.washingtonpost.com/politics/trump-foundation-ordered-to-stop-fundraising-by-ny-attorney-generals-office/2016/10/03/1d4d295a-8987-11e6-bff0-d53f592f176e_story.html?utm_term=.fedaa8d78cc6.

Fisher, Anthony L., "Hillary Clinton Likely Lost Because More Democrats Stayed Home." *Reason*, January 6, 2016. www.reason.com/blog/2017/01/06/hillary-clinton-likely-lost-because-demo.

Fox News, "FBI's Clinton Foundation investigation a 'high priority' among some agents, sources say." Fox News, November 2, 2016. Accessed January 23, 2017. www.foxnews.com/politics/2016/11/02/fbis-clinton-foundation-investigation-now-very-high-priority-sources-say.html.

Griffin, Taylor, "Three Ways Donald Trump Could Win." *Arc*, November 4, 2016. www.thearcmag.com/three-ways-donald-trump-could-win-this-election-b86be505e138#.xnndudkyf.

Gorelick, Jame and Thompson, Larry, "James Comey is damaging our democracy." *The Washington Post*, October 29, 2016. Accessed January 23, 2017. www.washingtonpost.com/opinions/james-comey-is-damaging-

our-democracy/2016/10/29/894d0f5e-9e49-11e6-a0ed-
ab0774c1eaa5_story.html?tid=ss_fb-bottom&utm_
term=.af163336828a.

Halper, Evan and Wilber, Del Quentin, "FBI says emails found
in Anthony Weiner's sexting scandal may have links to
Clinton inquiry." *Los Angeles Times*, October 29, 2016.
www.latimes.com/politics/la-na-pol-fbi-clinton-email-
probe-20161028-story.html.

Harris, Gardiner and Goldman, Adam and Martin, Jonathan,
"Obama Faults F.B.I. on Emails, Citing 'Incomplete Information'." *The New York Times*, November 2, 2016. Accessed January 23, 2017. www.nytimes.com/2016/11/03/us
/politics/obama-james-comey-fbi-hillary-clinton.html.

Jordan, Will and McDermott, Matt and McElwee, Sean, "4
pieces of evidence showing FBI Director James Comey
cost Clinton the election." Vox, January 11, 2016. www
.vox.com/the-big-idea/2017/1/11/14215930/comey-email-
election-clinton-campaign.

Maloy, Simon, "The Benghazi farce deepens: The GOP's conspiracy hunt is undermined from within." *Salon*, May 16,
2016. www.salon.com/2016/05/16/the_benghazi_farce_
deepens_the_gops_conspiracy_hunt_is_undermined_
from_within/.

Media Matters Staff, "David Brock: Manufactured Email
Scandal Part Of A 20 Year 'Campaign Of Legal Terrorism
Against The Clintons'." MMfA, August 11, 2016. www
.mediamatters.org/video/2016/08/11/david-brock-man-
ufactured-email-scandal-part-20-year-campaign-legal-
terrorism-against-clintons/212350.

Merica, Dan and Tatum, Sophie, "Clinton expresses regret for
saying 'half' of Trump supporters are 'deplorables'." *CNN*,
September 12, 2016. www.cnn.com/2016/09/09/politics
/hillary-clinton-donald-trump-basket-of-deplorables
/index.html.

Miller, Matthew, "James Comey fails to follow Justice
Department rules." *The Washington Post*, October 29, 2016.
www.washingtonpost.com/opinions/james-comey-
fails-to-follow-justice-department-rules-yet-again

/2016/10/29/3a2fad58-9ddd-11e6-b3c9-f662adaa0048_
story.html?utm_term=.ee1c9d9fb333.

Palmer, Thom, "Field guide to defending Hillary Clinton against
every fake scandal: email, Benghazi and more." Daily
News Bin, July 2, 2016. http://www.dailynewsbin.com
/opinion/field-guide-to-defending-hillary-clinton-
against-fake-scandals/24710/.

Palmer, Thom, "WIKILEAKS ESPIONAGE and the CLIN-
TON FOUNDATION." Thom Palmer Politics, October
27, 2016. www.thompalmerpolitics.blogspot.com/2016/10
/wikileaks-espionage-and-clinton.html.

Reilly, Ryan J., "Democrats Call For Probe Of FBI
Leaks About Clinton After Rudy Giuliani's Comments."
Huffington Post, November 4, 2016. www.huffingtonpost
.com/entry/fbi-leak-hillary-clinton-donald-trump_us_
581cece3e4b0e80b02ca024d?.

Rosenfeld, Steven, "Did Rogue FBI Agents Attempt Presidential Election Coup by Reopening the Clinton Email Investigation?." Alternet, November 4, 2016. www.alternet
.org/did-rogue-fbi-agents-attempt-presidential-ele-
tion-coup-reopening-clinton-email-investigation.

Sanger, David E. and Sheer, Michael D., "Putin Led a Complex Cyberattack Scheme to Aid Trump, Report Finds."
The New York Times, January 6, 2017. www.nytimes.com
/2017/01/06/us/politics/donald-trump-wall-hack-russia.
html.

Serwer, Adam, "Don't Let the FBI Decide the Election." The
Atlantic, November 2, 2016. www.theatlantic.com/pol-
itics/archive/2016/11/dont-let-the-fbi-decide-the-ele-
tion/506174/.

Timberg, Craig, "Russian propaganda effort helped spread
'fake news' during election, experts say." The Washington Post, November 24, 2016. www.washingtonpost.
com/business/economy/russian-propaganda-effort-
helped-spread-fake-news-during-election-experts-
say/2016/11/24/793903b6-8a40-4ca9-b712-716af66098fe
_story.html?utm_term=.397dc33af809.

Tomasky, Michael, "Trump: The Gang." The New York Review,

January 19, 2017. www.nybooks.com/articles/2017/01/19
/trump-the-gang/.

Tracy, Abigail, "HAS THE F.B.I. GONE FULL BREITBART?"
Vanity Fair, November 3, 2016. www.vanityfair.com/news
/2016/11/fbi-investigation-clinton-foundation-peter-
schweizer-breitbart.

Tracey, Michael, "Despite Donald Trump, Many Bernie Sanders Supporters Won't Forgive Hillary Clinton." *The Daily
Beast*, October 2, 2016. www.thedailybeast.com/arti-
cles/2016/10/02/despite-donald-trump-many-bernie-
sanders-supporters-won-t-forgive-hillary-clinton.html.

Trend Watch, "Clinton Says Half of Trump Supporters Are in
a 'Basket of Deplorables'." *Merriam-Webster*, September
10, 2016. www.merriam-webster.com/news-trend-watch
/clinton-says-half-of-trump-supporters-are-in-a-basket-
of-deplorables-20160910.

Witte, Griff, "Trump backers realize they've been played." *The
Washington Post*, October 4, 2016. www.washingtonpost
.com/news/worldviews/wp/2016/10/04/trump-backers-
feel-played-as-wikileaks-fails-to-come-through-on-oc-
tober-surprise/?utm_term=.cd1adee9be46.

Wright, David, "Poll: Majority disagree with not charging Hillary Clinton." CNN, July 11, 2016. http://www.cnn.com
/2016/07/11/politics/hillary-clinton-fbi-charges-poll/
index.html?campaign_id=A100&campaign_type=Email.

Yglesias, Matthew, "The real Clinton email scandal is that a
bullshit story has dominated the campaign." Vox, November 4, 2016. www.vox.com/policy-and-politics/2016
/11/4/13500018/clinton-email-scandal-bullshit.

Epilogue

Associated Press, "FBI Director Comey Faces New Investigation Over His Handling of Hillary Clinton's Emails." *For-
tune*, January 13, 2017. www.fortune.com/2017/01/13/
james-comey-hillary-clinton-fbi/.

Beinart, Peter, "Fear of a Female President." *The Atlantic,* October 2016. www.theatlantic.com/magazine/archive/2016/10/fear-of-a-female-president/497564/.

Blake, Aaron, "John Lewis says Donald Trump isn't a legitimate president, and Trump hits back hard." *The Washington Post,* January 14, 2017. www.washingtonpost.com /news/the-fix/wp/2017/01/13/john-lewis-doesnt-think-donald-trump-is-a-legitimate-president/?utm_term= .f64261b2f354.

Blow, Charles M., "No, Trump, We Can't Just Get Along." *The New York Times,* November 23, 2016. www.nytimes .com/2016/11/23/opinion/no-trump-we-cant-just-get-along.html?mwrsm=Facebook.

Goldman, Adam and Rosenberg, Matthew, "Democrats Confront F.B.I. Chief at Closed-Door Intelligence Briefing." *The New York Times,* January 13, 2017. www.nytimes .com/2017/01/13/us/politics/democrats-confront-james-comey-fbi-chief.html?_r=0.

Parks, Maryalice and Rogin, Ali and Siegel, Ben "House Democrats Slam FBI Director James Comey After Closed-Door Briefing." ABC News, January 13, 2017. www .abcnews.go.com/Politics/house-democrats-slam-comey-closed-door-briefing/story?id=44768462.

Reichmann, Deb and Sullivan, Eileen." *Portland Press Herald,* January 10, 2016. www.pressherald.com/2017/01/10 /angus-king-sees-the-irony-in-fbi-directors-refusal-to-confirm-or-deny-investigation/.

Reid, Joy-Ann, "Already Happening: Media Normalization of Trumpism." *The Daily Beast,* November 27, 2016. www .thedailybeast.com/articles/2016/11/27/already-happening-media-normalization-of-trumpism.html?via= desktop&source=facebook.

Remnick, David, "An American Tragedy." *The New Yorker,* November 9, 2016. www.newyorker.com/news/news-desk /an-american-tragedy-2.

Smilowitz, Elliot, "Trump rips John Lewis: Worry about your 'crime infested' district." *The Hill,* January 14, 2017. www.thehill.com/homenews/administration/314325-

trump-rips-john-lewis-worry-about-your-crime-infest-
ed-district.

Wagner, Meg, "Title." *New York Daily News*, January 13, 2016.
www.nydailynews.com/news/politics/donald-trump-
calls-hillary-clinton-guilty-hell-article-1.2945285.

Wolfgang, Ben, "Hillary Clinton's former spokesman questions 'legitimacy' of Donald Trump's victory." *The Washington Times*, January 13, 2017.www.washingtontimes
.com/news/2017/jan/13/hillary-clinton-former-spokes-
man-questions-legitim/.

Acknowledgments

When I began to follow Hillary Clinton's 2016 candidacy nearly two years ago, I was full of hope and excitement over what seemed the likelihood of her successful bid for the presidency of the United States. By the time I sat down to collect my blogs, notes, posts, and vast collection of articles in preparation for writing this book, I was in mourning, my work burdened by the weight of sadness and anger. In the months that followed, as the poisonous fictions that sunk Hillary's chances continued to be common wisdom, while at the same time as we were asked to accept as normal the nearly daily lies, cons, ethical violations and betrayals of human rights of the man who won, a fierce desire to tell what I saw as the truth of the election began to burn its way into my writing.

For helping me to sort out feelings and arguments, and for being a great friend along the way, my biggest thanks go to Sam Stoloff. Sam initially proposed to me how to best shape the book, and helped me to stay true to that vision, while empathizing with what was a times was a painful process of pruning away distracting asides and the vestiges of "real-time" Facebook rants. He was as much a discerning editor as a supportive agent, and whenever I wasn't sure what should go and what should stay—which was often—it was Sam I turned to, Sam whose judgment I trusted.

It was Sam, too, who suggested that Melville House might be a good home for the book, and that has proved true, both in MHP's enthusiasm for the project and in the assignment of editor Taylor Sperry, who helped further streamline and bring the narrative—which she rightly saw as having a tragic arc—to the fore. Taylor also helped crisp up my sometimes winding prose. I'm a writer who is more wedded to my ideas than my words, and I love it when someone else is able to say what I'm thinking more cleanly and elegantly than I can. Taylor often did that.

I owe a huge debt of gratitude to my research assistant, Adriana Sisko, for all the many and sundry tasks she performed—from researching topics to collating Facebook pages and preparing the bibliography to providing insights about millennial thinking.

To the community of bloggers and Facebook friends with whom I've commiserated, fumed, shared ideas, and from whom I've received so much encouragement for this project: Thank you, thank you! Your support has often kept me going when I was flagging. Special thanks go to Thom Palmer, a tireless truth-seeker and writer who collaborated with me on "Enough About the Damned Emails," a piece that originally appeared in *Huffington Post* and has merged organically with the "Damned Emails" chapter in this book.

To my current students, both my brilliant doctoral dissertators and the vibrant undergraduates in my media and culture class: Thank you for your patience, and for being so gracious about being abandoned during the last few months. I've learned so much from you, and your spirit, honesty, and intelligence give me hope in these grim times.

To my husband Edward: We've shared forty-four years of unfettered conversation about politics, literature, and movies—conversations in which we welcomed each other rants and raves about the state of the world, and during which your insights never ceased to amaze me. By now, your ideas and mine are so intertwined, have developed through such constant interaction that it's impossible for me to single out particular contributions. You are there in some way in every chapter of this book. And—no small achievement—you kept me balanced while I wrote for hours on end virtually every day, while my fingers cramped and my temper frayed. You let me shout when I needed to, you calmed me down (when it was possible) and you made me laugh. You are, quite simply, indispensible to me.

To my daughter Cassie: You always come to my mind when I see the currently popular feminist slogan: "Nevertheless, he persisted." But you don't need a printed tee shirt to "persist"; persistence is who you are and always have been, my resilient, clever, argumentative, beautiful girl, who persists in being Cassie no matter how hard they try to change you. Your strength and your individuality dazzle me and inspire me, and my love for you goes beyond anything I could have imagined. You light up the rooms of our home and my heart when you enter. And I see the future in you, and then—no matter how ugly and dark things may be now—the future lights up too.

Susan Bordo
Lexington, Kentucky
February 2017

Index

Index

A Note About the Author

Susan Bordo is a media critic, cultural historian, and feminist scholar. Her books include *Unbearable Weight*, which was nominated for a Pulitzer Prize, and, most recently, *The Creation of Anne Boleyn*. She holds the Otis A. Singletary Chair in the Humanities and is Professor of Gender and Women's Studies at the University of Kentucky.